The New Way To Design Your Own Website With WordPress

The ultimate, step-by-step, beginner's guide to a full-featured WordPress website for small business, consultants, authors & bloggers

NO CODING REQUIRED | SAVE EXPENSIVE DESIGNER FEES

NARAYAN KUMAR

new.designWPsite.com

Cover design by: Narayan Kumar

All sample content for use along with this book can be downloaded from the author's website: new.designWPsite.com/downloads
All help videos supplementing the instructions in this book can be viewed on the author's website: new.designWPsite.com/videos

Table of Contents

The New Way To Design Your Own Website With WordPress
i

1. Here's a map of your journey
1

2. Setting up WordPress locally
11

3. Getting to know WordPress
22

4. Customizing the About page
32

5. Global settings
56

6. Editing the Products page
65

7. Finalizing the Contact page
77

8. Creating a Blog (optional)
84

9. Editing the Home page
94

10. Must-have skills to learn
112

11. Making revisions
124

12. Migrating to the web
137

13. Finishing touches
147

14. Where to next?
157

May I ask you for a small favor?
160

Coming soon... Design Your Own Website With WordPress - Volume Two
161
About The Author
164

1. Here's a map of your journey

Welcome to your own website! And here we are at the very start of the build.

Today is reading day. You take it all in. You learn all the background stuff you need to know for a good grasp of the fundamentals.

Before you know it, you will be diving into the deep end. With my friendly guiding hand on your shoulder.

A quick word on WordPress

Think of WordPress as though it were Microsoft Word or PowerPoint. Like Word helps you make documents and PowerPoint helps you make presentations, WordPress helps you build websites.

WordPress is the world's most popular web builder. It is a popular piece of software that powers over 450 million pages. That is a lot of pages. It accounts for 43% of all websites. WordPress started as a simple blogging platform over 20 years ago. Today it is a feature-rich, flexible piece of software that can build virtually any kind of website.

What kind of a book is this? Does it tell you everything?

This is a hands-on guide to teach you skills that will save you big, fat designer/developer fees. It is a practical guide to website building, not a theoretical textbook.

Keep the guide open and execute the steps on your computer (not phone or tablet but on a desktop or laptop.) By the end of the book, you will have built a fully functional, secure, and feature-rich business website.

This is a practical, to-do book. Treat me as you would a friend who is good at something. I will lay a friendly hand on your shoulder and tell you only what's necessary. I will say, "Do this and then do this" and keep moving you along rather than stop at every little step and tell you every back story.

I think it's more natural to learn a new tool this way. To learn Powerpoint, for instance, you wouldn't painfully go through explanations of every menu item and sub-menu item in the app before making a single slide!

Yet I've seen beginner tutorials on PowerPoint that explain obscure little details without an overall context.

Our tool of choice for building a website, WordPress, is a free (but complex) piece of software. It can do a thousand things, for sure. Does that mean you have to learn all the thousand things before you can build your website? No way.

We have all visited countless websites. So we already know what a website should be all about. No rocket science there. We will apply this common sense awareness to arrive at a goal we are happy to reach.

Learning something new always feels strange. Once you get past that feeling, learning becomes pretty simple.

You don't need any prior knowledge of how websites are built to use this book. You probably know next to nothing about WordPress, the free software we will be using to build our site. It does not matter. And you certainly don't need any knowledge about coding and tech stuff.

WordPress, as noted, is the world's most popular software for building websites. Once you have a working knowledge of WordPress you can easily build a website for yourself (or someone else) with whatever features you have in mind.

All you need is a desktop or a laptop computer. No phones please. Not even a smartphone. Your computer can be a PC or a Mac, it does not matter. And you're good to go.

Who is this book for?

This book teaches you **how to make a website for a small business or a personal blog.** It is a step-by-step guide that you can personalize for your needs easily.

If you are any of the following, this book can help you in a practical and relevant manner.

- Consultant
- Yoga trainer
- Executive Coach
- Life coach
- Holistic medicine practitioner
- Therapist
- Blogger, writer or author
- Designer or copywriter looking to expand their skillset
- Landscaping service provider

- Plumber
- Dentist
- Financial Advisor
- Any professional who offers an online service through time slots
- A small business owner

You get the idea. **As long as yours is a small business and you are not selling products online**, this book is a perfect fit for you.

To be clear, this book is **not for e-commerce businesses** that sell products or services for money straight off the site. (What you will learn here are all the necessary steps for building *any kind of website*. It's just that an e-commerce site is an advanced, complex application that requires additional steps than are covered in this guide.)

Why build a website? Isn't social media good enough?

Since you purchased this book, you probably already know the value of a website. But let's discuss the key aspects quickly.

Social media content is a stream - a constantly changing landscape of fresh content replacing old content... of a few minutes ago! Beyond catching visitors in some random fashion, you aren't assured of the consistent exposure of your message. If you need consistent exposure, then you have to have paid ads on social media.

Are paid ads effective for your line of business? It is a debatable subject, but the costs are real and recurring. Difficult to sustain for small businesses, professionals, and bloggers.

Further, the content on any social media platform belongs to them, not you. If you publish something 'improper', the platform may even decide to ban you. Your content disappears, you cease to exist there. You don't own anything on social media including all the original stuff you put up there. Let's be clear on that.

On the other hand, **your website is your website from day one** and forever. Your content remains steady and visible to whoever visits, not a scrolling stream.

The best combination for building your brand is to **use streaming, transient social media to drive traffic to your permanent, stable web pages.** This can be powerful as thousands of businesses have discovered.

Why use WordPress to build? Why not Wix or Squarespace?

You may have heard of template sites like Wix or Weebly or Squarespace. They offer you a ready space for your website on the internet and also some ready-made templates.

Targeted at non-coders and novices, these sites give you pre-designed web pages from which you choose the one you fancy. You replace the sample content with your own (text, visuals, etc.), and - voila! - your website is ready.

You pay a monthly subscription. You don't need to know any tech stuff. These sites are easy to use for anyone looking for a quick and dirty solution for their business website.

There is nothing wrong with using such websites. But be aware of the limitations. Being template-based, you can choose the closest template that fits your business. But that's about it. Sooner or later, you may find it's not quite the perfect fit it appeared to be.

Besides, as with social media platforms, the content you create here will vanish the moment the company decides to leave the game. That may or may not happen, but who can guarantee that?

As some of my clients discovered (and then became my clients), you can get 'stuck' with template-based sites. If you outgrow the template there is no easy way to transfer your site elsewhere. You are locked in.

Finally, there is the monthly charge you keep dishing out.

By contrast, a WordPress site is based on free software. Barring a yearly spend on your domain name and domain hosting subscriptions, you pay nothing for the software itself.

(We'll get into domain name and domain hosting in later chapters.)

A WordPress site gives you ownership from day one. If you want to leave the game someday, it will be your call. No one else's.

It's easy to learn too. If you can do a slide presentation using software like PowerPoint, you can build a website using WordPress.

Obviously, the functionalities are more extensive and complex than slide presentation software, but they are not difficult to learn.

You are holding a book in your hands that promises a full website build starting from scratch with no prior knowledge. That in itself should tell you how doable this is.

Put aside an hour or two every day to learn the steps. And you'll have something built by your own hands for your own use with your own content talking to your own audience. In about two weeks.

Let's dive in.

What kind of a site are we building here?

We are building a website for small business. Very specifically, we are building a website for a small pharmaceutical firm. We will build a 5-page website that includes the following:

- A content-rich **Home** page (front page)
- An **About** page that talks of the expertise and origins of the company
- A **Contact** page so people can reach the company
- A **Products** page that displays the business offerings
- A **Blog** page to share the company's suggestions and health tips
- Along with a **common header** at the top of each page (including the navigation menu) and a **common footer** at the bottom of each page

We will have a solid, fully functional website at the end of it.

And, yes, I hear you say, but I'm not a pharma company! In fact, I'm not a company at all! I'm a plumber/landscaper/consultant/blogger. Why am I building a company website if I'm not one? Isn't it a waste of time and energy to be building something other than what I need?

Hold on to your horses. I'd be the first to tell you that there is nothing special about using a small pharmaceutical company for our purposes. I have no medical background myself (far from it!). But you know what? When we build something specific and concrete, we learn procedures and tricks in a practical manner.

Once we learn, we are in a position to apply the tricks to any other kind of website we want to build. A small business is very much like any other small business in many ways. All of them have products or services on offer which have to be displayed. All of them need an About page to talk of their pedigree. All need a contact page. Some need a blog as well.

All the text you need will be provided by me, so you don't have to write anything. As you will find out, I'm not a pharmaceutical expert but I've written out (fake) content for every page we'll be building and given you royalty-free images for use in each chapter to help you build something that feels like the real thing.

With the knowledge gained, **you will know enough towards the later chapters of the book to create a custom website for your business.** Just tweak the content and design to suit your own business. Add new features that your business needs. Delete stuff that your business doesn't need. (You'll know how to do all that by the time you reach that point.)

I strongly **recommend you follow my steps and build the same site in great detail along with me.** Don't skip details. Especially if you're new to WordPress, you will learn WordPress without getting sidetracked by having to create relevant content as well for each page. Plus if you lose your way it will be difficult to catch up because my screen displays will be different from yours. All the 36 SilentMoves videos I have for your guidance show the moves on the pharmaceutical website so that every reader and me are on the same page at all times.

So let me state it again. **Build the website that is being built in this book.** Step by step. Trust me, once we do all the steps, you will be ready to jump off and build yourself a unique, fantastic website for your business.

Note: If the idea here is to use a pharmaceutical firm's website as a template that you can tweak, then, hey, isn't that the same idea behind template sites like Wix? No, not really. The difference is that the template you choose from a site like Wix is the one **you use finally** with whatever features it has; whereas the small business template in this book is the **starting point to learn** to build whatever site you want. It's the difference between getting a ready-made sketch that you color in and getting a box of crayons to draw different things.

Once you've built all the pages with my guidance, you will know how to:

· build **pages**

- design **sections** within pages
- drag and drop **elements** (text, images, etc.) within sections
- **edit and revise** anything

That's the whole point of the book—teaching you how to custom-build with WordPress. We'll be using a theming plugin called **Elementor** extensively to do the heavy lifting, but we'll get to that shortly.

With the skills learned, **you can revisit the completed pharmaceutical website after Chapter 9 and reshape it into whatever you want.** You can add and delete stuff on every page depending on what matters to you. You can write and rewrite your copy as many times as you wish to get it perfect.

You can search for the perfect images that should feature on your website. You can browse YouTube for the perfect videos that serve your purpose.

You can change fonts and re-design layouts the way you wish.

It will all fall into place. Especially when you also have at your disposal a collection of **voice-free videos on my site that I call SilentMoves to follow all the mouse clicks and moves** mentioned in the book.

There are as many as 36 SilentMoves videos, brief and to the point, to help you complete the different tasks in the book. Taken with the text and the copious screenshots, you will have all the tools at hand to learn everything. Let's get hands-on then!

How different is this from my earlier book?

I re-wrote my earlier book **Design Your Own Website With WordPress** for the most part. The purpose of both the books is the same: to teach you to build a full website for yourself or business without coding or technical knowledge with WordPress. In that sense, they both do a good job.

What's the difference, then? **The main difference is building a new site on the web right away (earlier book) versus building it in your own computer and later uploading it to the web (this book).** I believe this is a simpler alternative for everyone.

Instead of straightaway deep diving into the complex world of web hosting, domain name buying and related online issues—these are important issues but have nothing to do with learning WordPress—the beginner is now inducted into the main job of building a website with WordPress using his or her computer. I have found and highly recommend a free piece of software (more on this later) that helps you build a website on your computer first without having to buy and own some hosting space on the web already.

Once the site is built, as noted, you can convert it into something specific for your business or interest. **We will then migrate your finished, polished local site to its permanent online home** on the web. We will handle and master whatever jargon that will come our way then. This way, all the non-WordPress issues of getting a site online come later on rather than at the beginning. Which, I think, is easier to deal with by a non-technical learner.

The other important difference between the earlier book and this one is that we built a site for a career coach then. We will be building a site for a small pharmaceutical firm here. So the approach, the actual steps and the final results are all totally different. If you want to learn how to create a site for a consultancy service as well as one for a small company making physical products, feel free to get the other book too.

Note: In the next chapter, we will be **setting up WordPress on your own computer** in readiness to start building with it. So onward!

◆ ◆ ◆

2. Setting up WordPress locally

L et's start with the first step. Let's install WordPress. We will be installing WordPress locally on your own computer. PC or Mac doesn't matter. But a minor digression is necessary here to clear out the confusion some of you may have.

The two flavours of WordPress

This may come as a surprise to you. There is one flavour of WordPress available at wordpress.org and another available at wordpress.com. What is this about? Which one should we use?

If you go to wordpress.org, you'll be able to download a free download of the WordPress software and install it in your own web hosting space (we'll get to web hosting later in the book)—or, as we're about to do, install it inside our own computer.

If you go to wordpress.com, you can't download anything. You'll find that the WordPress software is already pre-installed there. All you can do is buy some space there and build your WordPress site on that platform itself. It is pretty much like going to Wix or Squarespace or similar template website and building your site on their website. You don't get to download anything, you just start building with what's there already.

Wordpress as a piece of software is the same more or less on both these sites. What differs is the manner you get to use it. Either you download it for free and build your own site wherever and however you want. Or pay some money for pre-installed WordPress and build a site (with some restrictions) on their site itself.

We will be taking the **free download option from <u>wordpress.org</u>** and building our own website, first on our own computer and then transferring the completed site to a web hosting platform of our choice. In practice, as we will see shortly, there is no need to even download WordPress ourselves. The enabling software that will help us set up WordPress will do the download for us behind the scenes.

Digression over.

Local by Flywheel

Flywheel is a premium web hosting company that has created a helpful, enabling piece of software called **Local by Flywheel** to easily install WordPress on your computer and build sites with it.

Local by Flywheel does the entire job of installing WordPress, including downloading it and activating it. So really speaking, you get a default WordPress website at the click of a button. Let's install Local by Flywheel.

Go to **localwp.com** and right on the home screen, you will see a download button or two. Click on it. After you fill up some details, choose your platform., PC or Mac. The download starts.

Remember you are not downloading WordPress, you are downloading an enabling software called Local by Flywheel.

Once downloaded, you can grab the Local by Flywheel icon and put it inside the Applications folder. It's much like installing any regular software on your computer, nothing different. And you're basically done.

Open the Local by Flywheel app by double-clicking the app icon. It opens to something like this.

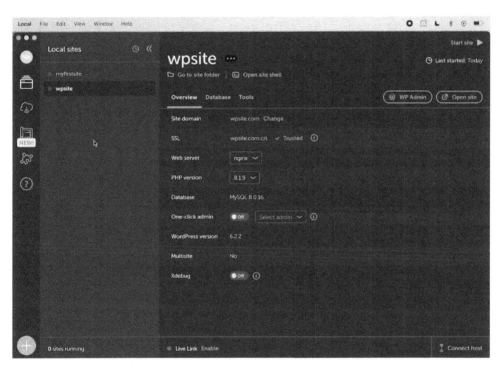

Since I have a couple of sites already on Local by Flywheel they show up here in the left column. Ignore them. Your screen will be empty. You will see a message saying you have not created any websites yet— something you can heartily agree with for it happens to be true. A button underneath asks you to create a new website.

Once you click on the button you can **create your first website in WordPress.** You are given two options: create a new site and create from a blueprint. Leave it at 'Create a new site' and click on 'Continue.' Give it a name 'mywordpress' and click on 'Advanced options' link below. In the box, check that the name reads 'mywordpress.local.' If it ends with '.com' instead, change it to the '.local' ending. Click on 'Continue.'

The next choice you have to make is between preferred options and custom. Keep to the preferred options and continue.

It now asks you for the WordPress username. WordPress is not yet installed but it will use the username you provide when it shortly installs it. The credentials you put in here will serve as the credentials for the WordPress website you're creating.

So put in your username and give it a password. Remember to fill in the email box with your real email. Don't leave it at default. Put in your actual email address here and then click the 'Add site' button.

Now Local by Flywheel goes to wordpress.org and downloads the WordPress software. It may ask you for the system password to install WordPress and in a few moments that should be done. Your computer now has WordPress installed in it and it all happened so softly and invisibly.

You now have two buttons that are important.

One is the **WP admin button** and the other, the **Open Site button.** If you click the Open Site button, your browser opens up. And you see the front end of your website 'mywordpress.local', which is basically an empty website. 'Front end' means the regular website view a visitor sees. It sounds professional and fancy. And, frankly, there is nothing much to see here—yet.

On the other hand, if you click the WP Admin button within the Local by Flywheel app, your browser opens up a new window showing the WordPress login screen. Put in your username and password to access the back end of the site. 'Back end' means the secret place where you and you alone wander to create and endlessly revise your website. It's the engine room where you fire up a brand new website from scratch, invisible to anyone else in the world. You work in the back end. People see the front end. What's more, you can also alternate your view from back end to front end and back whenever you wish, how many ever times you wish.

To enter the exciting back end world of WordPress, fill in your credentials in the login box that shows up in the browser. (Want to watch a step-by-step help video on how to install WordPress in your computer? Go to new.designWPsite.com/videos and watch **Video #1 Install Local by Flywheel.**)

WordPress now greets you with a welcome screen. This may be slightly different from the one shown below, depending on when (time of year) you login. The version numbers and the welcome graphics change every few weeks, but you are well and truly at the back end of WordPress.

WordPress calls this initial screen as the **Dashboard**. On the left is a black column with menu items. As the course progresses, we will be using

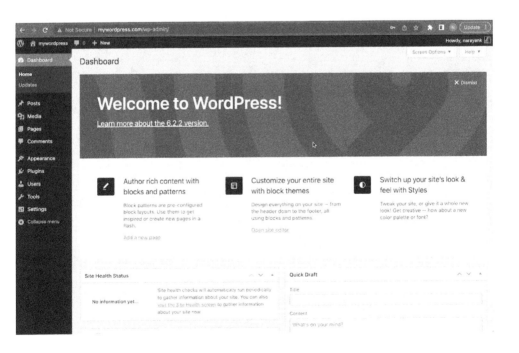

these items and getting to know them better. For now, we don't need to get overwhelmed by everything we're seeing here.

This is your welcome screen and we will learn how to clean up and start. What I want you to know is that since we are at the back end, there is a direct way that we can get to the front end without going via Local by Flywheel. Hover your mouse in the top left corner where we see 'mywordpress', our site name, and click on 'Visit site' that appears.

On the front end, as noted, there isn't much to see. But I want you to notice that next to the left of the address bar it reads 'Not Secure.' See image below. It's a sign that says your site is not safe. Not safe against malware or spam or bad bots of the web. Which is not a good thing.

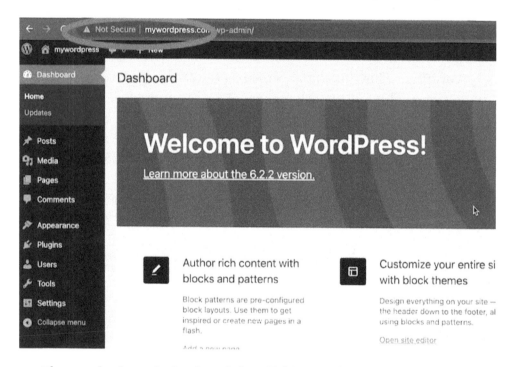

If we go back to the back end (by clicking in the same top left corner) the address bar still reads the same. The browser is telling you there is something important we must address almost as soon as we've begun our WordPress journey.

Getting an SSL Certificate for security

Local by Flywheel helps us to **get an SSL certificate** and make the site secure.

Never mind the geeky stuff of what this certificate is all about. All we have to know is that we need an SSL certificate to protect our site from all the evil baddies of the online world. You cannot have a non-SSL site these days on the web. It is true that your site currently only exists on your own computer and no one else can visit it. Just like no one else can see your photos or documents on your computer unless you post them or mail them, no one can see the Local website you build on your computer.

True enough, but at some point we will be transferring the site or sites that we make inside our local computer onto the web. It's good practise to get into the habit of making our site SSL-safe right from the start.

Local by Flywheel makes the process of getting an SSL certificate pretty easy. **It's done in 2 steps.** One, you make a small adjustment in Local by Flywheel software. And two, you make another small adjustment in the WordPress site on our browser. Follow the steps below or watch a short, silent movie that explains the moves: go to <u>new.designWPsite.com/videos</u> and watch **Video #2 Make it ssl-safe.**

Step One: Look at the Local by Flywheel app screen. In the list of items, you'll see SSL listed among the top few. See the green button that says Trust alongside? Click on it. If it asks you for your system password, enter it. Step one, done.

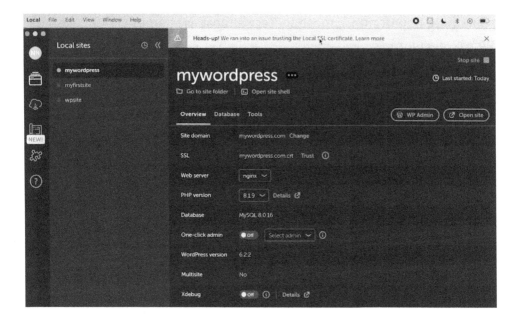

A minor digression: If you see an error during Step One...

The error message (shown at the top of the Local by Flywheel app as a 'heads-up') is something that appears on some Mac computers. Click on the 'Learn more' link at the end of the message line itself to figure out how to correct the error. The instructions are clear enough to follow even if they don't carry any particular meaning for you (as with so many computer-related instructions.) If you don't see the above error message, your Step One is done and you can move on.

Digression over. Let's move to Step Two.

Step Two: We go from the Local by Flywheel app to our browser, and specifically, to the back end of our website that should already be open. Look for 'Settings' in the left, black column somewhere near the bottom.

Click on Settings to see a sub-menu under it (General, Writing, Reading, etc.) Click on General. Fill in the site title box with 'My WordPress.' At least for now. We'll change this to your real business name once we've learned all the tricks. Fill in the tag line box with 'Learning

WordPress.' Filling in these boxes, incidentally, has nothing to do with the SSL certificate business we came here for. We're doing it because we happen to be here.

Now to get to business: the SSL issue, step two. What you really need to do is to change the value against the WordPress Address (URL) box. This should be already filled in with 'http://mywordpress.local'. Now add an 's' after the 'http' so that it reads 'https://mywordpress.local'. In the box below that says Site Address (URL), do the exact same thing.

All you've done is change 'http://' into 'https://' in two places. Believe it or not, this makes your site secure! Go to the bottom of the page and click the 'Save changes' button. The moment you do that, you'll get logged out. Don't worry, it was meant to happen. So login again. And look on top at the address bar now.

The non-secure message is gone. Instead, you should see a tiny symbol. If you click on it, you should see 'Connection is secure.'

Trust me, I understand your perplexity. None of us regular folks fully get why doing these two steps makes our site SSL-secure. But it does. It's a good thing. It makes us happy. And it's behind us now.

Onward!

Let's make a couple of **clean-up tweaks** to the Settings since we are here. Click on Settings in the left column of your WordPress back end screen, and this time instead of General, click on the third item, Reading. (From now on, the changes we initiate will be to do with WordPress rather than general, computer-related gobbledegook like SSL.)

On the Reading page, go to the bottom and **click on the checkbox** against the line 'Discourage search engines from indexing this site.' While you're building this site, you don't want Google or Bing or any other search engine to index your site. Besides, it's going to be a fictitious pharmaceutical firm's site in any case for now. Why would you want its contents to be read by Google and methodically indexed? When your real site is ready and complete, you'll come here to uncheck this box. Till then, we'll keep the box checked. Click on the blue 'Save changes' button below.

Make one more change. Look under Settings again in the left, black column and click on Permalinks. On this page, the permanent structure can be one of many options listed. Your job is to make sure the 'Post name' option is the chosen one. If something else is chosen, change it to 'Post name.' This is important. Click on the blue 'Save changes' button. You're done. For now.

Chapter summary

• We downloaded Local by Flywheel from localwp.com.

- You set up SSL in two steps: by clicking on the Trust button within the Local software and going to the site's back end Settings > General to change http setting to https
- You watched a couple of videos: Video #1 and Video #2 at https://new.designWPsite.com/videos
- You ticked the box at the bottom of Settings > Reading page
- You selected the 'Post name' option in Settings > Permalinks page

These are the initial settings for your WordPress site. Congratulations, you have a working WordPress site in place right now!

◆ ◆ ◆

3. Getting to know WordPress

We jumped in at the deep end and installed WordPress software in your computer using another piece of enabling software Local by Flywheel.

Diving into WordPress: Let's clean up

Let's get back to your WordPress site to continue the good work. Make sure Local by Flywheel is running and you've clicked on the site name 'mywordpress' in the left column. Now click on the WP Admin button. You will be taken to the back end of your website via the login page.

From here on, we'll let Local by Flywheel run on in the background and forget all about it. We'll focus on developing our WordPress site in our browser. Just remember, if you switch off Local by Flywheel for any reason, your WordPress site will stop working.

So, here we are at the WordPress back end, the Dashboard page—staring at a visually noisy and talkative page that we've seen before. This back end view, only visible to you because you logged in, is also known as the **admin view.** This is the basic, vanilla WordPress welcome page, the same that thousands of others see upon installation.

I don't know about you, but I find all the information boxes on this Dashboard page distracting, crowded and not making sense. At this early stage in our learning curve, we can do with less distractions and less intrusive stuff. Let's de-clutter the Dashboard page.

Click on the little tab in the right top corner which says **Screen Options**. See screenshot below. Click on it for a hidden section to drop down, where you find a few items listed next to check boxes. Untick all of them.

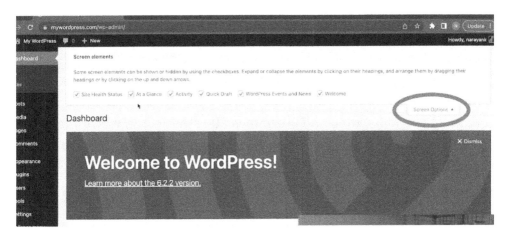

Click on Screen Options again to close the dropdown. You now have a very clean Dashboard. Let's proceed with a few other clean-ups to the Settings section. Look for **Settings** in the left, black column and click on **General** under it. When it opens, you will recognise it. You've been here before to change 'http://' to 'https://'. You also filled in the Site title and the Tagline. Remember?

We'll make one more tweak on this page in the Timezone box. The default value shown—UTC plus zero—may or may not be your zone. If you scroll up you'll find above the UTC options a listing of representative cities in each zone. Look for the city that represents your time zone. Click on **Save changes** button at the bottom of the page.

Now look for **Plugins** in the left column and click on it. We'll be discussing plugins (along with themes) in detail and using them in a bit. For now, just notice that this page is empty. We have no plugins installed. Which is all good for the moment.

In a similar vein, there is a page for Themes, which is another page we must clean up. Again, never mind what themes are and what they do, we'll address those shortly.

In the left column, you will NOT find an item called Themes. But you will find an item called **Appearance**. Hover your mouse on it and a sub-menu shows up with **Themes** as the first item. Click on it.

On the Themes page, there are three themes already installed with the leftmost one being the active one. WordPress comes with these default themes to get you started and are named after the year in which they were released. You're not obliged to use them. You would 100% of the time find your own theme rather than use these basic default themes.

WordPress cannot run without a theme. Some theme has to be active always. And **no more than one theme can be active** at any given moment.

So, given the clean-up binge we are in currently, we can get rid of the two other themes which aren't active. Hover over one of the **non-active theme boxes** and click on Theme Details which shows up. Look for the red Delete link at the bottom and click it. Click again on OK to confirm.

That's gone. Similarly, delete the other non-active theme. Now you're left with only the active theme. In an upcoming lesson, we will be replacing this theme too. But for the moment, it's all good.

You've cleaned up the themes page.

A word about WordPress themes and plugins

Here we go. What are they, these plugins and themes, exactly? Why do you need them?

Plugins are bits of software that either expand or add functionality to the basic WordPress software. They 'plug in' to the mother software and make it better.

For instance, WordPress is already capable of handling the image needs of your site. However, there are dozens of plugins (mostly written by third-party folks, not connected with the company that makes WordPress) that can give you some amazing and additional image editing and handling capabilities.

Again, if you want to make your website multilingual and make it appear in the visitor's language as they log in from different parts of the world, WordPress by itself cannot do the chameleon dance in real-time. Thankfully, if that's your requirement, there are specialist plugins that can get the job done for you.

Where do you find these plugins and how do you go about installing them? We will be doing it quite a bit in this book and you will see how simple the process is.

There are thousands of WordPress plugins out there—a big reason for the immense popularity of WordPress itself—and many of them are free. For others, you have to pay an annual subscription. (We will be using only free ones in this book.)

Themes are also bits of software but with a different purpose—to 'decorate' the site with styling. There are hundreds of them out there—some are paid, and many are free.

One main difference between themes and plugins is that you generally have multiple plugins active on your site to help out with various

functionalities, but you can have only one theme active at any given moment.

Themes too have to be installed on your website in much the same way that plugins are installed.

We will go ahead and install a free and popular theme called **Astra**, as well as a plugin called **Elementor** (which is crazily a plugin that does the theming! But more on that shortly.)

There is a useful plugin called **Starter Templates** that does a wonderful job of installing itself as well as both the Astra theme and Elementor plugin at one go while offering us a host of templates to design our pages.

(There is a paid version of this plugin Starter Templates with a gazillion more templates and features but for our purposes, the free one will do.)

And now to **install our first plugin** that will in turn install the plugin and theme we need.

Installing the Starter Templates plugin

Normally speaking, plugins are plugins and themes are themes. The former for functionality, the latter for styling. But there are a handful of plugins like Elementor that do the styling job of a theme. These go by the name of 'page-builder plugins.'

Since every WordPress site needs a theme that is unambiguously a theme, Astra will do the job for that. Once we install Elementor, it will play well with Astra and generally take over the actual theming of the site in a major way.

If you're asked later what you used to build your site with, you will say, 'Elementor' even though you have Astra installed. It's the way it is.

Back to our narrow black column on the left. Look for 'Plugins' and hover. Click on 'Installed plugins' in the sub-menu that appears. The page that shows up is blank as we've noted before. Click on the **'Add New'** button on top of the page to the right of the title 'Plugins'.

You are now on a repository page (on the massive WordPress site) of plugins. Thousands of free plugins live here and we head to the search box on the top right and **type in 'starter templates'** and wait for a few moments.

The first one that heads the listing is the one we want: Starter Templates by Brainstorm Force. It has a good star rating by a few thousand people, 1+ million active installations, and was last updated recently.

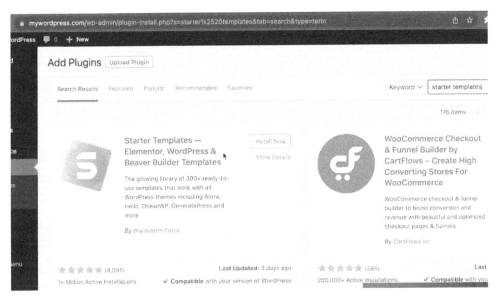

This stuff - **star rating, number of people doing the rating, number of installs, and the last update date** - will come in handy to judge the usefulness and safety of all later plugins we install. The better the numbers, the better you will feel about installing them. They have been crowd-tested on your behalf.

Now click on the 'Install Now' button. Once Starter Templates is installed, the button changes to read **'Activate.'** Click on it. You'll be taken to your plugins page where the Starter Templates plugin is the sole item in the list. It is now installed and activated. (Either that or the Activate button turns into an un-clickable grey Active button. If so, click on Plugins > Installed plugins in the left column.) As simple as that, you've gone and installed your first plugin.

Watch the installation of Starter Templates plugin as a help video at https://new.designWPsite.com/videos. Look for **Video #3 Install Starter Templates**.

Using Starter Templates to create a template

The whole point of Starter Templates is that it gives you many design templates to choose from. It lets you find and **use a ready-made template for your website as a starting point.**

If you hover your mouse over the Starter Templates name in the plugins page, a sub-menu appears beneath the name. See screenshot below. Click the 'See Library' link.

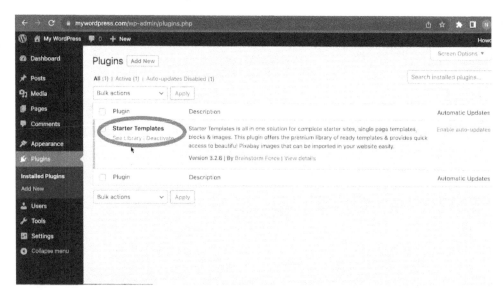

You are now given a choice of three page builders to select from: WordPress's own page builder (called Gutenberg, by the way), Elementor and another popular page builder, Beaver Builder. **Click on Elementor.** The question asked of you now is: What type of website are you building? The Library has many templates of websites to choose from.

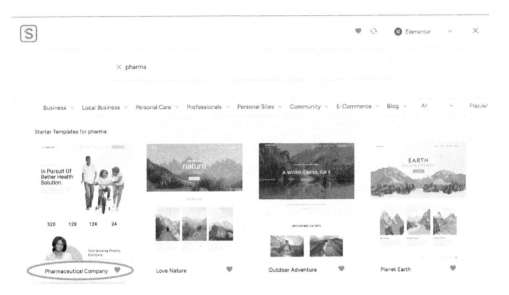

Let's choose a template for our imaginary pharmaceutical firm. Click in the search box and type 'pharma.' In the choices that show up, click on 'Pharmaceutical company.' See screenshot above. In the couple of screens that follow, you get to decide on some basic choices for theme colors and fonts.

(Because of the endless tweaking you can do, you'll come to realize that you can practically take any template and make it do your bidding. **So don't get too choosy or go necessarily by the name of a template.** We'll proceed with the 'Pharmaceutical company' template in any case, since this is our first time here.)

In the left column, it asks you to upload a site logo if you wish. We can do this later. Click on the 'Skip and Continue' button to the next page which lets you change the default colors used by the theme. Below that, you are shown a few font pairings (one font for headlines and another for body text) that you can choose from.

Keep the Color Palette to Original. Choose the **Roboto Condensed-Roboto font combination**, which is an elegant pairing. You can always come back later to change things around.

Click on the 'Continue' button at the bottom of the page. Fill in your name, email, and a couple of other details. I normally uncheck the box that says 'Share Non-Sensitive Data'. Click on the 'Submit & Build My Website' button.

The Starter Templates plugin now goes about installing itself in addition to other things we need for our site: the Astra theme and the Elementor plugin. When it's done, click on the 'View Your Website' button.

Note: For click-by-click video guidance in real time, **watch Video #4 Install pharma template** at new.designWPsite.com/videos. There's no distracting voice-over, only mouse clicks to clearly show you how to set up and install the pharma template.

There it is—**an entire website filled out with dummy content.** You can scroll down the front page to see all the different sections one below the other. You can click on any menu item on top to go to other pages on the site. Go through the pages and see the uniformity in design and color.

We have a full website for a small pharmaceutical business using all typical features a website needs—including a multi-section home page, an about page for the firm's expertise and history, and a contact page with relevant details. All are styled in the site colors and site fonts we chose earlier. No template however good will exactly fit a real firm's business needs. We will now learn how to modify the content (text and images) on every page to suit our firm's exact needs.

I advise you to stay in step with me in the following chapters. Do the steps I do, and make the sections and pages exactly the way I recommend. It will help you stay grounded. We have a long distance to go in this book. *It makes sense that your site and my site march forward in an identical fashion at every step of the way and we both end up on chapter 9 with the same result.*

Note: For copyright reasons, I will be using images that I have either shot myself or have the permission to use. These will replace the free ones from the template. You are free to use my images in your test site. Or, you can download royalty-free images from sites such as pexels.com, unsplash.com and pixabay.com (explained shortly).

Let's **start with the About page** in the next chapter.

Chapter Summary

- You cleaned up the Dashboard page
- You deleted all themes except the active one on the Themes page
- You learned about the differences between a theme and a plugin
- You installed Starter Templates, Elementor and Astra
- You chose the pharma company template and its colors/fonts
- You watched the **SilentMoves Video #3 Starter Templates install** and **Video #4 Install pharma template**

❖ ❖ ❖

4. Customizing the About page

PREPARATION: To use the sample content for use with the About page, download the aboutpage.zip file from here: new.designWPsite.com/downloads

Before we edit the About page, it's good to know if we're logged in to our site or not. How do we know that? Look at the space at the very top of your site, whichever page you happen to be on. If you see a slim, black band with some words on it - especially the words 'Howdy, username' on the extreme right - you are logged in.

If you're saying, "What black band are you talking about?", then it means you're logged out. To log in, start up Local by Flywheel and select 'mywordpress' in the left column. Click on the WP Admin button. You will be taken to a browser page—specifically, the login page of your website. Enter your WordPress credentials and get in. Now you're logged in.

Incidentally, to log out of your site, click on the 'Howdy, username' link at the extreme right of the thin, black admin bar on top of the screen. From the dropdown menu, click on 'Logout.'

It always happens that when you log in, you get taken to the back end of the site. Click on the extreme left of the admin band on top (yes, that same slim, black band) which has the name of your site. You'll be taken to the front end. Good.

Note: To look at the **finished version of our about page** on your site, visit: new.designWPsite.com/about. This is the filled-in content and look we are aiming for.

The role of Elementor, Astra & Starter Templates

Before we proceed with the About page edit, let's have a brief review of the roles of Elementor, Astra and Starter templates. What does each do? We have to be clear about that.

First, **Elementor is a popular plugin**, a page builder for theming WordPress sites. This will theme 90% of our site, so we will learn a lot about Elementor and how to use it. It's our main focus. You can say this course is basically a WordPress-Elementor course.

Second, **Astra is a theme**. In fact, it is a full-fledged theme in its own right that you can use solely to build a website. Since we will be using the page builder Elementor to do the heavy lifting for us, Astra's role in building our site will be minimal. It's as if the only reason we have Astra at all is because WordPress needs a theme and cannot function without one. Besides, Astra will come in handy to complete the 10% bit that Elementor (free version) cannot do. More of this later.

The good thing is Elementor and Astra work well together behind the scenes. So, even though we'll get to work with Astra, its role in our course will be much diminished because we will rely more on Elementor to get theming tasks done.

Starter Templates is also a plugin like Elementor. Its job is to offer us many ready made designs for use with Elementor (as we saw earlier.) By choosing our Pharma theme, we have already made use of this plugin and don't have to worry about it much any more.

Editing the masthead of the About page

Fire up Local by Flywheel if you haven't already. Click on WP Admin button to login to your mywordpress.com in your browser. Get to the front end by clicking on the site name in the top left corner.

You'll see the Home page as given to us by the Starter Templates plugin. From the main menu section on top of the page, click on the 'About' link. The About page shows up with its various sections already designed for us. Scroll down and take a look at everything on the page.

Since no template, however good, will ever be perfect for our own specific needs, we are going to learn how to **edit the About page and its sections.** We get to know how to take a given template and make it bend to our will in ever so many ways.

Learning how to **add, revise, replace or remove sections** (and elements within sections) is the skill we need to build a page to our liking. So let's

The About page brief

evermed

Home   Company   Products   R & D   Contact   Call Us: 123 456 78 90

Our Company

Semper tellus, tellus at eu platea lorem est a amet tincidunt
nulla orci vulputate tellus felis

- Display 4 famous products with a link to the Products page

- A section on the two directors with photos

pretend we are building the About page from what it is to what our client, Sapphire Pharma, wants it to be. Look at the client's brief above.

The first three points have to do with the **masthead section** of the About page. Let's address them first.

The 'client' wants a new headline and a new background image to replace the ones already there. And they want to add a call-to-action button that isn't there. If we get these 3 things done, the masthead is done. And we can move on to the next bullet point.

Remember that the slim section at the very top of the page (with the logo on the left, the main menu and a green button on the right) is NOT the masthead section. It is called the header section which we will handle later.

Why later? Why not now? Because the header is something that repeats on all pages of a website. It is not exclusive to the About page. It can be

edited from a central place later, once and for all, to change it throughout the entire website.

Onto the masthead section. Even though it's difficult to see the exact boundary between the masthead section and the header section above it—they have been artfully overlapped—they are indeed two different sections as we'll shortly discover.

To edit anything on the About page, you have to be on the About page on the front end first. Since we are there already, click on the 'Edit with Elementor' link in the black admin band on top of the page.

We now find ourselves in the **Elementor Edit version** of the About page. See screenshot above. The actual content covers most of the page with an Elementor column on the left for making our edits. Whatever changes we carry out in the Elementor column will be instantly executed in the page content.

Between the two columns, midway vertically, there is a small rectangle with a left-facing arrow. Click on it to remove the Elementor column momentarily so that you see the page content occupying the entire screen area. Click on that arrow again to get back to editing the page. It's a neat mechanism to check your handiwork as you make progress.

The Elementor column displays its 'elements' or 'widgets' - like heading, image, text editor, icon, button, etc. As and when required we will drag any of them onto the main page.

Turn your attention to the content part occupying most of the page, especially the masthead section and what's within it. Let's try and edit what's there to suit our whim.

When you **hover your mouse within the masthead section away from any words in the section,** a pink border encases the section with a pink 'crown' on top with three icons - a plus, a cluster of dots and an 'x.' See screenshot above.

Click on the middle icon - the cluster of dots - **to select the masthead section.** Watch the Elementor panel on the left change instantly. (Incidentally, the 'x' sign deletes the section and the '+' sign adds a new section. But we won't go there yet.)

The Elementor panel changes to help you edit the section. The words on the top band now read 'Edit Section' (or 'Edit Container', depending on your version.) Below that are various editing controls. See the screenshot on the left.

This is the main way of working with Elementor. First, you click on something within the content part of the page—a section, a headline, a text box, an image, etc.—and then edit that something inside the Elementor panel.

You'll get the hang of this as we work our way through the page.

Editing the masthead section

We are already in the Edit mode of the masthead section.

We can **change the background image** of the pale graphic in this section to an image of our choice. I have given you the image titled masthead-about.jpg. In the Elementor panel on the left, click the middle button right on top that says 'Style.' In the Background section, click on the image that's already there in the Image box.

You'll be taken to the WordPress Media Library, a place where all the images used in the site are stored. Drag the image masthead-about.jpg from your desktop (or wherever) and drop it inside the Media Library window. Once the image is added, select it by clicking on it. Click on the 'Insert Media' button at bottom right.

The new image should show up in the content area now, replacing the earlier background image.

Note: As a background image, this image should cover the whole of the masthead section. Sometimes you may get a result not quite covering the whole space and to one side. If this happens, look for the Position setting under the image in the Elementor panel and select 'Center Center.' Also change the Display Size setting to Cover, if it isn't that already. The image in the content panel should now behave itself.

Click on the pink UPDATE button at the bottom. Click the tiny, left-facing arrow on the dividing line between the two panels on the page to make the Elementor panel go away. View the page in its entirety. Click on the same arrow to get back to editing.

Let's **change the headline text**. We want the new headline to read, 'The Company That Cares' instead of the default 'Our Company.'

To change the headline text, click somewhere within the headline in the content panel. The Elementor panel changes its mode to 'Edit Heading.' You can see it says so in the top band.

A Title box also shows up below. Type 'The Company That Cares' in the box after deleting what's there. **Click on the pink UPDATE button at the bottom of the Elementor panel. Note its position.** You'll keep returning here time and again to save your work. Important!

Let's **change the subheading** too underneath the main heading. Go to the sample content pdf you downloaded for this chapter. Copy the subhead text. Now click anywhere within the subheading box in the content panel. The Elementor panel now shows 'Edit Text Editor' in the top band. Replace the text in the text box by deleting it and pasting in the text from the pdf. Notice the text changes in the main content panel. Click on the pink UPDATE button below.

Adding a button

So far, we replaced what was already there - the background image, headline and subheading. But we don't see a button that can be replaced. How do we add something that's not already there?

Like **adding a button** under the subheading, for example.

To add a CTA (call to action) button, we need the Elementor panel to be in its 'elements' mode rather than the 'edit' mode that it is in currently. Click on the cluster of nine dots in the Elementor panel. It's in the top band to the right of where it says 'Elementor'. This is not the earlier cluster of 9 dots on top of a section; this is a similar looking one in the Elementor panel. Clicking it displays the elements or widgets.

Since a button may not be among the visible widgets, type 'button' in the search box. The button widget will come into view. Drag it over to the main content just under the headline 'The Company That Cares' till a pink horizontal line shows up. Let go. You'll see a button appear under the headline with the default text of 'Click Here.'

Click somewhere within the button area. In the Edit Button column of Elementor that now shows up on the left, fill in 'GET IN TOUCH' in the text box against the word Text. The button is already styled and when I hover over it, it changes to a green patch with white lettering on top which suits us fine.

Fill in the **link box** with '/contact' without the quotes so that when someone clicks the button, it will take them to the Contact page.

Click on the green UPDATE button at the bottom to save your work thus far. **To get out of Elementor** and view the page as a visitor would view it, **click on the hamburger icon** (three lines one below the other) in the top band to the left of the Elementor panel.

From the menu that appears, click on 'View Page.' It will take you to the front end of the About page.

The masthead section of the About page is done! It has a revised headline and subhead, a new background image and a brand new button that wasn't there to begin with. You have taken small but decisive steps.

Need some video help to follow along? Go watch the **SilentMoves Video #05 - Edit masthead of About page.** At: new.designWPsite.com/videos.

There's more to be done. More sections await your editing. To continue your work, click on the 'Edit with Elementor' link on the black admin bar on the front end.

The About page brief

- A background image in the masthead
- A headline that says "The Company That Cares" to highlight the corporate philosophy
- A CTA (Call To Action) button in the masthead to contact the firm
- A section on the founder with his photo
- A section on innovation
- Display 4 famous products with a link to the Products page
- A section on the two directors with photos

Editing the Founder Section

According to the client's brief for the About page, what follows the masthead should be a section on the founder of the firm. For this section, they've given us a headline and some body text to go with it (you'll find it in aboutpage.pdf download file) and a photo of the founder, founder.jpg.

When we look at the **section of our template** that follows the masthead, it looks promising. There is some bold text we can replace with our headline and a bunch of text matter that we can replace our own body text. There is mostly blank space on the left, where we can easily add our founder's photo. See screenshot below.

Need some video help to follow along? Watch the **SilentMoves video #06 Founder section of About page.** At new.designWPsite.com/videos.

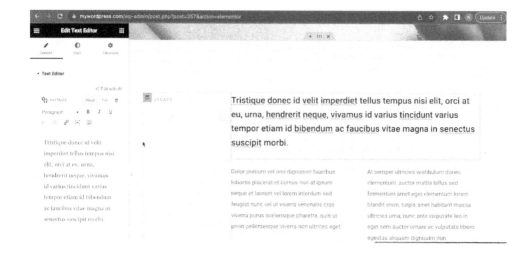

Let's get to work. To place our main heading, click on the bolded text. In the Elementor Text Editor box in the left column, select all the words and delete them. See screenshot above. Copy the new headline from the pdf and paste it in the box: 'Our founder's vision of improving lives...' Click on the pink UPDATE button below. In the main content area, you will see the new headline in place.

Click somewhere inside the text below the headline. In the Elementor panel, you will see the Text Editor with the current copy in it. Copy the paragraph text from the chapter pdf and **replace the existing paragraph text** with the copied one. Click on the pink UPDATE button below.

Watch the main content section of the page update itself with the new custom text. The tiny subhead of 'At a glance' to the left of all the text matter does not make sense in our context. Let's replace it with 'Our legacy.' Click the text in the content panel. In Elementor panel's Text Editor, replace the old text with new text.

We can now go about displaying the founder's image in the blank space underneath the 'Our legacy' line. I've given you the image founder.jpg in the download folder.

To insert an image, as noted before, we need Elementor to be in its 'elements' mode rather than its 'editing' mode. Click on the cluster of 9 dots on the top bar to the right of the word 'Elementor'.

You will see the elements or widgets, one of which is Image. Drag the Image widget onto the empty space underneath the subheading and let go.

You will see a placeholder image in the Elementor panel. Click in the image box, and from the Media Library import the founder's image. You can do this by clicking the 'Upload files' tab on the top left and using it to upload the downloaded image from your computer into the Media Library.

Click the 'Insert Media' button at the bottom right to display it on the page. The image is too big for its column and overflows into the text column. In the Elementor panel, click on the 'Style' tab on top. Drag the Width slider to the right to 70%. Look for the Border Radius section a little down the panel. Fill in 12 in the leftmost box and it will auto-fill 12 in the other boxes too. This makes the corners of the image curved rather than sharp. Now click on the 'Content' tab on top of the panel. In the Alignment setting below the image, choose the leftmost icon to align the image to the left. And we are set.

Our founder's vision of improving lives has always been our guiding principle

20 years ago, Late Ramesh Marfatia was very unhappy that small towns were so underserved by pharma companies. It became his burning mission to make sure that all small towns had access to medicines. That was the genesis of Sapphire Pharma. Today the company serves over 121 cities with 150,000 doctors prescribing our products. The trust that we enjoy with millions of consumers has been built with absolute dedication, town by town, one street at a time. It is no small feat that building and preserving this trust is what has lead us to become a $2.3 million powerhouse.

The About page brief

- A background image in the masthead
- A headline that says "The Company That Cares" to highlight the corporate philosophy
- A CTA (Call To Action) button in the masthead to contact the firm
- A section on the founder with his photo
- A section on innovation
- Display 4 famous products with a link to the Products page
- A section on the two directors with photos

There's a help video to guide you. Watch the **SilentMoves Video #06 Founder section of About page** at new.designWPsite.com/videos. There's no distracting voice-over, only mouse clicks to clearly show you how to edit the page.

Click the pink UPDATE button as always. Open up the screen to full width to see your handiwork so far. The Founder Section (as well as the masthead) is now complete.

Before we work on the next section—which, according to our brief is the Innovation Section—we notice in the template that we have a counter section that we have no use for. That gives us an opportunity to learn how to delete a section.

With the Elementor panel open, scroll down the content panel so you get to see the counter section clearly. Moving your mouse in the section (not too close to the numbers, though) will give you a pink bounding box around the section with a 'crown' on top with the dotted icon and an 'x' icon as before.

Since we don't want to select the section but instead get rid of it, click on the 'x' icon. Poof. The section is gone. Let's move on.

Editing the Innovation Section

The next section that is titled by the template as 'Fast Growing Pharma Company' is a useful one that can be easily re-purposed as the Innovation Section we want. In the download file for this chapter, you will find all the material you need to copy and paste: subhead, headline, body text, quote, name and designation. For the image on the right, we will use an image that the template already has in the WordPress Media Library.

Let's begin the edit by scrolling down to the section that is just below the Founder's section and select the subheading 'Our Company' by clicking on it. As before, we use the text box in the Elementor panel to copy-paste the new subheading 'A bigger tomorrow'. Similarly we replace the current headline below the subheading by selecting it and replacing the words in the text box with 'Innovating for growth.' (The new text matter is given in the download for the chapter.)

By now, you know how to change existing text with new text, whether that's a heading or body text. The procedure is exactly the same. Select the line or para in the content panel and type in or paste in the new text in the box in the Elementor panel. Click the UPDATE button and move on.

Copy the body text paragraph from the pdf and replace the body text below the headline in a similar fashion.

Copy the quotation text from the pdf and replace the quotation text in the content panel. (You can delete the quote marks at the beginning and

end of the text because we do have a stylistic big, green quote mark to the left as also a name and designation below.)

Select the name of the person below the quote. That is a small but separate element in itself. Fill in the new name in the text box in the Elementor panel to replace it. Do the same thing with the designation text below. Select it and type in the new text.

We'll leave the signature in place and pretend it's the real thing. This is incidentally an image, not text. (So if you want to replace it you'll need an image of someone's signature and brought in as an image. For now, let's stick with what's there.)

You can by now see how repetitive the process of bringing in new copy can be! It's really the same thing done over and over. And before you know it, the whole of the left column in the Innovation Section is done and dusted. The right column is an image. The client does not want a company person there; they want a science-lab type photo that represents expertise and innovation.

Click on the lady's image. The Elementor panel changes to show 'Edit Image.' An inset box shows up a tiny version of the image already there. Click on the tiny image. You get taken to the Media Library. You will notice

I haven't given you an image to use in the download for this chapter. That's because the image we seek is already within the Media Library.

The pharma template we chose happens to have a relevant image to suit our purpose. It's named pharma-company-template-product-img.jpg. Click on it once you find it. Click on the select button at bottom right of page. It will get inserted in the page layout as shown below.

In the Elementor panel, click the middle tab on top that says 'Style' and enter '12' in any of the four Border Radius boxes. Since the values are linked, entering a value in one box changes the values in the other three boxes as well. And we get our curved borders on our image that we've defined for ourselves as a consistent standard.

Got that done? You've finished this section. Close the Elementor panel out. You remember how to do it, right? Click on the tiny left-facing arrow in the vertical dividing line between the two panels on the page.

The image in the right column is way too up in relation to all the text in the left column. Let's bring down the image by increasing the empty space above it. **Aligning elements** is a handy skill to have.

Open up the Elementor panel by clicking the tiny arrow again. Click on the tab on top which says 'Advanced.' It's our first visit to this tab. Things like spacing are tackled here. We want to change the spacing on top while keeping the spacing on the other three sides intact.

Before you enter a value, make sure that the last icon in the row, which is the link icon (circled in red in the screenshot above left), is not 'pressed in'. That interlinks all the values and makes them the same when you enter one value in a single box. You don't want that. Click on the link icon to unlink the values. Now enter '100' in the Top box. That keeps the other boxes at zero. And, more important, the image in the content area moves down the page and looks more balanced with the other elements in the section. Click on the UPDATE button one final time for this section. Go to the far left at the very top of the Elementor panel and click on the 3-lined hamburger icon there. In the menu that appears, click on 'View Page.'

You'll be back on the front end of the About page. Scroll down and up to admire the work you've done so far. The masthead, Founder's Section and the Innovation Section are all done. And the unneeded Counter section is nowhere to be seen. All good so far, then. Onward.

If the above instructions are tedious to follow, watch the **SilentMoves Video #07 Innovation section of About page** at new.designWPsite.com/videos to see how simple this really is.

Editing the Products Section

We now come to the Products Section which is a question of displaying the firm's 4 famous products (images) and have a link underneath to the

The About page brief

- A background image in the masthead
- A headline that says "The Company That Cares" to highlight the corporate philosophy
- A CTA (Call To Action) button in the masthead to contact the firm
- A section on the founder with his photo
- A section on innovation
- Display 4 famous products with a link to the Products page
- A section on the two directors with photos

Products page where all their products would be displayed with brief descriptions.

We notice that under the Innovation Section we just finished, there is a section titled 'Neurology & Oncology'. Our pharma firm has no use for this section. Click on 'Edit with Elementor' on the black band on top of the page to start working the page with Elementor.

Hover your mouse within this section, wait for the pink border to appear, and click on the 'x' on top to get rid of it. Do the same with the video section below.

The next section on the page looks promising. It's titled Awards & Recognition and has two rows of four columns each. We just need space for our 4 products, so we can delete the bottom row. Hover your mouse over the bottom row of four columns and right click on the column icons to delete them. This leaves us with an outer column that was 'holding' the 4 inner columns. Right click on the column icon at the top left and delete the outer column too.

Click inside the headline 'Awards & Recognition'. In the Elementor panel, we can replace the text in the Title box with 'Our famous products.' Click on the Style tab on top of the Elementor column and click on the leftmost icon in the Alignment line to left-align the headline (it's currently in the center while the rest of the page is basically left aligned.)

Now turn your attention to the images in the content panel. Click on the first image. In the Edit Image Elementor panel, click on the thumbnail image and import the 4 images into the Media Library as before. The download folder contains the product images: apitone.jpg, decolic.jpg, duo-LS.jpg and effectal.jpg. You can drag them all into the Library in one go and click on apitone.jpg to select it and click on the Select button at bottom right to insert it in our page.

In similar fashion, bring in the other 3 images in each of the remaining columns. Once all are in place, click on the first image again. In the Elementor panel, click on the 'Style' tab at the top. Go to the Border Radius part towards the bottom of the panel and enter 12 in one of the boxes to make them all 12. The image gets its curved borders as per our style.

There is a shortcut to apply the border radius settings to the other three images. Right-click on the pencil icon in the right top corner of the first image and from the menu that appears, click on Copy. Now, right-click on the pencil icon in the corner of the second image and from the menu, click on Paste Style. The border styling is applied instantly. Do the same with images 3 and 4.

The brief requires us to add a link below the images to the products page. We will do it once we finish the Products page. Get out of Elementor for now and View Page to review the work done so far. Watch **SilentMoves video #08 Products section of About page** at <u>new.designWPsite.com/ videos</u> to get the hang of creating the Products section.

The About page is nearing completion with the masthead, Founder's section, Innovation section and Products section already in the bag. Just the Leadership section remains.

Editing the Leadership Section

So far we built all our sections by looking at the existing sections in the template and editing them to suit our needs. We face a new problem now. With the Leadership Section, we find we have reached the footer part of our template. The green section along with the 3 sections below together form the common footer of the site, found on all pages of the site.

You'll see the problem for yourself when you click on 'Edit with Elementor' to get back into Edit mode. If you scroll down the content panel, you'll find that below the Products Section there is nothing for us to edit or repurpose. The footer sections don't show up at all here because, as noted, they don't 'belong' to the About page alone. They belong to the

The About page brief

- A background image in the masthead
- A headline that says "The Company That Cares" to highlight the corporate philosophy
- A CTA (Call To Action) button in the masthead to contact the firm
- A section on the founder with his photo
- A section on innovation
- Display 4 famous products with a link to the Products page
- A section on the two directors with photos

entire website and have to be edited in a central place elsewhere, not in the About page. What now?

Let's **create a new section from scratch!** What you do see at the bottom of the content panel is a set of three icons—a plus sign, a folder icon and the Starter Templates icon. The plus sign adds a fresh, new blank section... yay, but wait. The folder icon adds a fresh new section using a ready-made Elementor template... which is better, but wait. The Starter Templates icon adds a Starter Templates template for a new section. Now we're talking. Click on this most promising third icon.

This takes us to a page full of Starter Templates templates. There are two tabs on top: Pages and Blocks. Click on Blocks, which is another word for what we've been calling Sections. From the dropdown menu at top left, click on Team. You'll get a few template options.

I preferred the second template (see above screenshot). Click on it to see a close-up view. It has a provision for a photograph, name, designation, descriptive text and social media links besides a general headline and description on top. It has 4 columns for 4 people and we need only two, but the extra ones can be easily edited out. Click on the blue Import Block button on top.

The new section is now in place below our products section. To get rid of the last two columns, hover your mouse in top left corner of the third

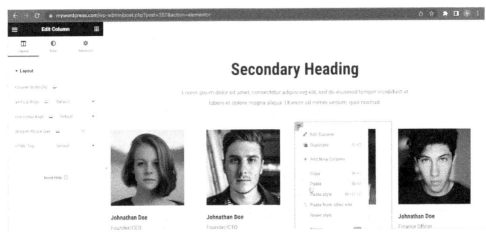

image from left. Right click there. See screenshot above. And from the dropdown menu that appears, click on delete. This will delete the entire column with all the elements inside it. Do the same with the last column.

Click on the heading on top. And revise it in the Elementor panel to "Vision for the Future." Click on the UPDATE button below. Since we don't need the description text below the headline we can delete it. Hover your mouse over the text then right-click on the pencil icon in the top right corner of the bounding box. From the dropdown menu, click on Delete.

Now for the images. When you click on the image, the Elementor panel does not read 'Edit Image'; instead, it reads **'Edit Image Box.'** What is an Image Box now? This too is an 'element' or 'widget' that Elementor gives us just like heading, text editor, button, etc. This is a composite widget in that it is a combination of an image, a title and a descriptor rolled in one. So the name below the image and the description below the name are also part of the Image Box. It is a handy one for use cases like bios, teams, leadership, etc.

In the Elementor panel, you can select the image as usual by clicking on the image thumbnail. Use the image in the download folder for the chapter. You can also fill in the Title and Description boxes with the copy given in the downloaded file. Click on the UPDATE button as ever to save your work.

Below the Image Box in the content panel, there is a regular text box. Click on it to select and in the Elementor panel, fill in the new text given to you in the download file. UPDATE.

The line has a row of social icons. Click on any of them. The Elementor panel shows 'Edit Social Icons.' This is another useful widget, a popular feature of modern websites. You can see the three widgets under Social Icons. Clicking on any of them reveals a Link box where you can put in the social media link to that person. Right now there is a # in the field, which is a customary thing to do when you don't yet have the actual link.

Presumably, when our fictitious client gives us the links, they will feature here. So, basically, we leave the social icons the way they are.

In similar fashion, work the second Image Box and the text below. Remember to save the work by clicking the UPDATE button. Get out of Elementor edit mode by clicking the hamburger icon and choosing View Page. And there it is... the entire About page is ready!

Congratulations, you have created your first multi-section, content-rich web page using WordPress and Elementor. The pharmaceutical company thanks you for the tremendous work you've put in. Watch the **SilentMoves Video #9 Leadership section of About page** to see how this section is created.

Chapter Summary

- You learned how to log in and log out of your site
- You put in custom text for the headline
- You changed the background image
- You added a button
- You edited paragraph text
- You added an image to the main section
- You deleted unwanted sections
- You left-aligned text
- You added a new section
- You used Image Box and Social Icons widgets
- You watched the video help for the sections with **SilentMoves Videos #05 to #9** over at <u>new.designWPsite.com/videos</u>

◆ ◆ ◆

5. Global settings

PREPARATION: Use the sample content with the Services page. Download the global.zip file from here: <u>new.designWPsite.com/downloads</u>

Before we proceed with our next page, the Products page, let's take a brief detour into global settings.

We have to activate certain settings that affect the whole site globally and not just this page or that.

Remember that this chapter on **global settings** does not apply exclusively to any specific page. The settings apply to the entire site and so to all pages of the site.

Global settings: Placing our logo

Global settings are those settings that affect the entire site at one go.

Changing global settings in the header or footer is done using the Astra theme rather than Elementor. The free version of Elementor does not do headers and footers. This particular pharma template we are using does an unusual thing of having a regular footer but instead a set of 4 blocks together as a 'footer': the green block at the bottom of every page, the 2-column block of logo + text below it, the 4-column text block below and the copyright message block at the very bottom of the page.

This 4-part footer in itself is not that uncommon. Many sites have it these days. But the fact **we have to edit the top two blocks in Elementor and the bottom two blocks in Astra** is uncommon.

Incidentally, barring such instances of global settings to be done inside of Astra, we will not be dealing much with other Astra settings in this book.

Let's **change the logo** in the header—something that affects the entire site. From the front end of any page, **click on 'Customize'** next to the site name on the black admin band on top.

As you can tell by the screenshot on the left, this is not the Elementor Edit page that we used before. This is the Customize Page of the site theme Astra.

Click on 'Header Builder' in the left menu. Now click on 'Site Title & Logo.' Click on the 'Change Logo' button. It will take you to the Media Library.

Here you can upload the SapphirePharma.png logo from the download folder for the chapter, using the 'Upload files' tab on the top left.

Click on the 'Select' button at the bottom right to insert the selected logo onto the page. If the logo takes up too much space, then drag the Logo Width slider in the Astra panel to the width you want. A value of 170px worked fine for me. Click on the blue Publish button on top to save the change. At a later stage, we will make a change to the main menu alongside the logo, but for now, we are done.

Note: For click-by-click video guidance, watch the **SilentMoves Video #10 Global settings: Logo** at new.designWPsite.com/videos. It will show you all the moves discussed above to set up the site logo.

Global settings: the footer section in Astra

Click on Customize in the admin bar to get back into the Astra back end. Click on 'Footer Builder' this time. To edit the bottom two sections of the footer, hover your mouse over the 4-column section first. You will see little white pencils in blue boxes pop up here and there. One pencil is for editing the entire section of 4 columns and the other four pencils are for editing the stuff inside each column.

In the three bands of white that you see below the columns, hover over

the widget in the leftmost column and click the 'x' to delete the widget. See screenshot above. But why are we deleting this? Because the pdf for this chapter download says the first column should contain some copy and not a menu.

Copy the text for column 1 from the global.pdf you downloaded. It's the text that begins, 'SapphirePharma is a fictitious pharmaceuticals firm... ' We need a new widget to paste this copy into. Click on the '+' in the space where the earlier widget was. Choose the HTML 1 widget. Click on the widget. Paste the copy in the text box in the Astra panel. See the **SilentMoves Video #11 Global footer with Astra** at new.designWPsite.com/ videos.

The second column has the widget for displaying a menu but it's not the menu we want. Click on the widget in the second column. In the Astra panel click on the menu that appears. Make the title 'Company' instead of Facilities and select the menu 'Primary Menu' from the dropdown.

The third column of 'Renal care, packaging, etc.' doesn't make sense for our website. Grab hold of the gear icon of the widget in the third column and move it across to the fourth column. The basic idea is to interchange the widgets in the third and fourth columns. See the help video to follow here. Once done, delete the fourth column widget as before by clicking its 'x' symbol.

The column is gone but the remaining 3 columns can be spaced out better. Click on the gear icon on the far left of the middle white band (circled in red in the screenshot below.) In the Astra panel, under Column choices, the setting is for 4 columns. Click on 3 instead. And in the Layout choices, click on the second one. The gap adjusts itself.

Let's look at the bottom-most section of the footer which is the one that holds the copyright message and social icons. In the bottom white band, click on the leftmost widget that says 'Copyright' (but not on the 'x' alongside, you will delete it!)

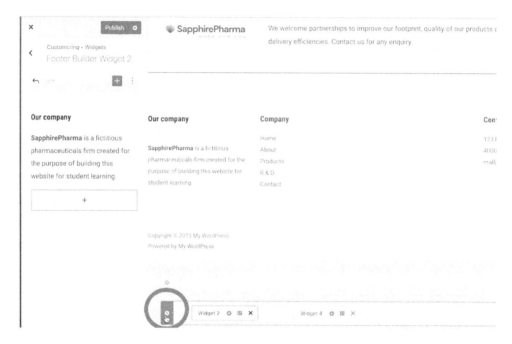

Let's understand what's going on here and see what we can influence. The Astra panel on the left displays an edit box. The text in the text box reads Copyright © [current_year] [site_title] followed by Powered by [site_title] in the next line. Here's your first glimpse of some WordPress code!

Don't worry. It should be simple enough to make sense of. The words inside the square brackets are dynamic code—**they enable WordPress to pull in the value of the current year as also the site title and display them without you having to type them out.**

With each passing year, the copyright year displayed will change automatically. Neat, right? Similarly [site_title] gets replaced by the site name you gave in the WordPress settings.

Let's get back to the bottom white band once more. Click on the button that reads 'Social.' You'll see in the Astra panel a listing of three popular social media. You can add more by clicking the blue 'Add Social Icon' button. Clicking on any of these in the list reveals a URL box which you can fill in with details from the client. Add a LinkedIn button if you wish.

We're done here. The last two footer blocks, which will appear on every page of the site, are complete. Remember to click on the blue Publish button on top of the Astra panel to save your changes. And click on the 'x' next to the Publish button to close the Astra panel.

Scroll down any page to make sure the bottom two footer blocks appear the same everywhere. To get all the moves right, you'll probably need to watch the **SilentMoves Video #11 Global footer with Astra** at new.designWPsite.com/videos

Global settings: the footer section in Elementor

As noted, there are two more blocks in the 4-part footer section. These two are controlled by Elementor. From the front end—it doesn't matter

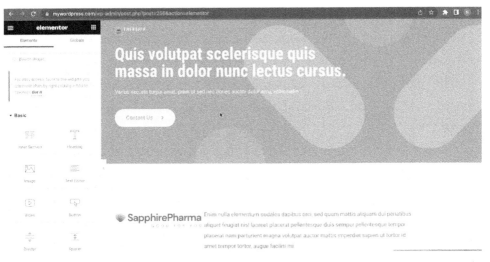

which page you're on because the footer is common to all pages—hover your mouse over Edit with Elementor link in the black admin band on top. Don't click on it. In the dropdown menu that appears click on Footer.

This opens up like any other Elementor Edit page we've seen before, except it shows only the two footer sections in the content panel and nothing of the page content. We see the top two footer block, the green one and the 2-column block with the logo on the left. See screenshot above.

Editing this is very much the way we edit anything in Elementor. Start with the subheading on top of the green block which reads 'Partnership'. Click on it. Copy the relevant text ('Building trust') from the pdf download for this chapter and paste it in the Edit Heading box in the Elementor column. Click on the UPDATE button to save.

Click inside the main headline and use the Title Box to paste in the new headline from the pdf. Save the change.

Similarly, edit the body text under the main headline. Copy the text from the pdf download and paste it in the text box.

The Contact Us button remains the way it is, so the button is ready for use. We don't have to do anything to it. Also the green background image featuring graphic pills also suits our purpose as a pharma firm. We can keep it the way it is. All in all, the green block of the footer is done.

What remains is the block below: the two-column block with the company logo image on the left and some text on the right

The logo image size is too big. Click on it. In the Elementor panel, click on the Style tab and adjust the width slider to 80%. Click on the UPDATE button.

Copy the right column text from the pdf download file. Click on the text in the content panel. Paste the new text in the Text Editor in the Elementor panel. Close out the Elementor panel by clicking on the arrow between the panels. All is looking good about these two footer blocks, except the white space below the green block seems excessive.

Open out the Elementor panel. Hover over the 2-column, white block to make the pink border box appear. Click the 9-dot selection icon on top of the section. In the Elementor panel, click on the Advanced tab on top. In the top Padding value fill in 70. That should cut the excess spacing in the white block. Remember to UPDATE.

Close Elementor by clicking the hamburger menu on top left and from the dropdown menu, click Exit. That takes you to the Dashboard at the back end. Watch the **SilentMoves Video #12 Global footer with Elementor** to follow all the clicks to get this section done.

Click on the site name at the top left of the screen in the admin band to take you to the home page front end. Scroll down to check the footer blocks below. All four of them should be in place. Go to a couple of other pages by clicking on the main menu. The footer blocks (as well as the header with the company logo) should be well in place.

Our global settings are done.

Changing 'Company' in the Main Menu

There is a small thing we can get done while we're managing global settings. There is this word Company featured in the main menu. We can change it to About because, let's say, that's what the company wanted us to do. And it gives us an opportunity to learn how to do stuff like this.

Click on Company in the main menu. Once you're in that page, click on **'Edit Page' link** on the black admin bar on top. This is a new link we're clicking on for the first time. We've used 'Edit with Elementor' before and we've used 'Customise' too to get into Astra.

The new link takes us to the barebones WordPress Edit page, un-styled by Elementor. Change the title from Company to About in the title box.

Now, in the right column, look for and click on the address link next the term URL. A box opens up showing 'company' as the permalink. Replace 'company' with 'about.' Click anywhere outside the box to make it go away. The URL value has now changed to 'mywordpress.com/about'—which is what we want.

Click on the blue update button on top right of the page to save the changes. A black band appears towards the bottom of the page where you can click on the View Page link. You'll get to the front end of your website. And you will notice that the main menu now has an item that reads About rather than Company. Watch the **SilentMoves Video #13 Global settings: Menu item** to help you get the job done.

Chapter Summary

- You learned what global settings are
- You used Astra to change the site logo
- You used Astra to change two footer blocks
- You used Elementor to change two more footer blocks
- You changed a menu item with WordPress
- You watched **SilentMoves Videos #10 to #13**

◆◆◆

6. Editing the Products page

PREPARATION: Use the sample content with the Products page. Download the productpage.zip file from here: <u>new.designWPsite.com/ downloads</u>

Planning our Products page

It's good to start with the brief before we build a page. A client, whether it's someone else or our own self, will have a fair idea of what they want to cover on any specific page of their website.

Our pharmaceutical firm wants the following on their Products page:

· Their product line, comprising 9 medical products, is the main reason for the Products page. They have to be showcased with photos and text

· The masthead should carry the headline and an interesting background image as also a call-to-action button

· There should be a general overview below the masthead along with a photograph ahead of the main products section

I will be providing you the text as usual in the chapter download as also most of the images barring one (deliberately so, more on this shortly.)

Let's get on to our site and do a quick audit of the template site. If you're starting a fresh session, then make sure Local by Flywheel is running, you've clicked on the site name in the left column and the WP Admin button near the top right of the app.

Once inside the back end of your WordPress site, get to the front end by clicking on the site name on the top left of the black admin band. You know all this stuff by now, of course.

We notice on the main menu an item already named 'Products.' Let's see what that page has to offer us. We know what the client brief wants us to do. Can some sections be repurposed? Should some sections be deleted? Does any new section(s) need to be added?

Click on Products in the main menu. The masthead on top of the page can be repurposed for sure. We can edit the headline and body text to suit our needs. We can easily add a CTA button (like we did in the About page.) And we can change the background image too. Great.

Then comes a section of copy that is sub-titled 'Overview.' This too can be reused by changing the headline and the text underneath. The number counter in the right column serves no purpose for us. We can delete it and use the column space for the image they wanted next to the overview text. Great, again.

All the rest of the sections below (till we reach the 4-part footer) are not lining up with our requirements. We need the rest of the page to showcase our line-up of our 9 products. The existing content doesn't do that at all. So we'll delete these sections and create a new one to house our product displays.

So there's our broad strategy for the Products page: revise the top sections, delete the remaining sections, and create a new section.

Editing the masthead section

Click on the 'Edit with Elementor' link in the admin bar above.

Let's make a few familiar and easy alterations. Let's change the words of the headline. Click on the headline. In the Title box in the Elementor panel, type in (or paste) the new headline: Our Products.

Similarly, change the text under the headline. Click on it and in the Elementor panel, paste the new copy from the pdf download for the chapter.

Let's add a button below the body text. In the Elementor panel, click on the 9-dot cluster icon to the right of the words Edit Button in the black band on top. That shows all the elements or widgets at your disposal. Drag the Button widget over to the content panel. If you don't see the Button widget, use the search bar above to type in 'button.' When you drag the widget over, you will see a pink line appear under the body text. Let go. You'll get a button with the default text of 'Click Here.' In the Elementor panel, against the Text line, type in 'Call us' to change the button text. Your page, thus far, should look like the screenshot below.

Onto the background image. Let's change the background image here to something I've given you in the chapter's download folder, masthead-products.jpg.

In the content panel of the page (not the Elementor column), hover your mouse in the masthead section and click on the Edit Section icon (the middle icon with 9 dots at the top of the pink bounding box.)

In the Elementor Edit Section (or Edit Container, depending on your version) column, click on the 'Style' tab on top. Click on the Image box below. It will take you to the Media Library. Click on the 'Upload files' tab on the top left and select the masthead-products.jpg from your computer.

Once uploaded, select the image and click on the blue 'Insert Media' button at the bottom right to place it on your page. As a background image, this image should cover the whole of the masthead section. Sometimes you may get a result like the screenshot below: not quite covering the whole space and to one side.

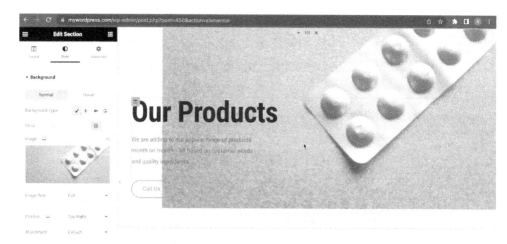

If this happens, look for the Position setting under the image in the Elementor panel and select 'Center Center.' Also change the Display Size setting to Cover, if it isn't that already. The image in the content panel

Over three decades of dedicated service through our quality products have earned us the trust of doctors, chemists, stockists and consumers across states.

Some of our well-recognised brands include Efectal suspension, Apitone syrup, Sneezy suspension, Klobat, Duovent and Sapridom.

300+
PRODUCTS

20
DOSAGE FORMS

32
THERAPEUTIC AREAS

128
PATENTS

should now behave itself. Click on the pink UPDATE button at the bottom. You can click on the little eye-icon to the left of the UPDATE button to preview the page with the changes done so far. This will open the site in a new tab. Useful trick to see the whole page without leaving Elementor.

The masthead looks fine but… the section 'bleeds' on to the header section above and obscures the menu. This pretty much happened in the About page as well. But we'll correct it this time. Get back into the Elementor browser tab and select the masthead section. In the Elementor panel, click on the Advanced tab. Unlink the values of the Margin by clicking on the rightmost link that looks like a link and unsetting it. Then enter 80 in the Top box. That pushes the masthead section down, clear of the header section. All is neat and well now. UPDATE.

Watch the above instructions in action. See **SilentMoves Video #14 Edit masthead on Products page** at <u>new.designWPsite.com/videos</u> to edit the masthead.

Later on, as we progress, we'll get to revising minor details. Like making the text under the headline more legible as also the button. Both are looking weaker visually right now than they should be.

Editing the Overview Section

The next section below the masthead is the Overview Section. The subheading in green already says that. So we'll keep that in place.

Click within the bold text below the subheading. In the Text Editor box that appears in the Elementor panel, paste the new text from our pdf download for the chapter.

Similarly, click within the paragraph beneath the headline. In the Text Editor on the left, delete the existing text and replace it with the downloaded text for this chapter (copy the text under 'Smaller text.')

The counters in the right column are not things we need. So hover your mouse over the first row of counters and click on the 'x' that shows up in the top of the section. See screenshot above. That deletes that row. Similarly delete the bottom row of counters as well. **Note: Depending on when you're doing this, you may not see the section as shown in the screenshot. In which case you're using a later version of Elementor that does away with 'sections' as a terminology altogether and replaces it with 'containers.' Watch the SilentMoves Video #15 Edit Products: overview section** at <u>new.designWPsite.com/videos</u> to learn how to delete the counters.

We are going to place an image in the now empty right column. This is something, unlike previously, I have not given you. I've downloaded a free image from a site called <u>pexels.com</u> and this is something you'll have to learn as a separate skill in your overall armoury of skills.

Go to <u>pexels.com</u> and in the search box put in 'pharma test tube' or similar. From the ones you see, choose one you like—it should be horizontal in orientation to fit our layout. When you get to the free download page, click on the green button that gives you various size options for your download. Choose the Small option. That will be good enough for an image that is not even half the width of a web page.

We'll be talking about image optimization at length later. Right now, just know that smaller the image size, the faster our web page will load. (And Google likes that very much, which is a good thing.)

Back to our Products page, Overview section. Click the '+' sign inside the empty right column. The Elementor panel will change to display all its elements or widgets. Drag the Image widget over to the empty column and drop it. Click on the thumbnail image in the Elementor panel to load up the image you downloaded from pexels.com.

Warning: Don't use any image you find on Google. Most images on the internet are copyrighted and not meant for free use. You can only use what are called **public domain images** where the author of the image has given you explicit permission for use. It's difficult to know which images are in the public domain and which are not. Thankfully many websites offer royalty-free images for your use. Some of the well known sites are pixabay.com, unsplash.com, and pexels.com among others. Feel free to use any of them.

With the image I chose from pexels.com, my finished Overview looks as below. You can use an image 'scientific' or 'medical' in a similar way.

OVERVIEW

Over three decades of dedicated service through our quality products have earned us the trust of doctors, chemists, stockists and consumers across states.

Some of our well-recognised brands include Efectal suspension, Apitone syrup, Sneezy suspension, Kiobat, Duovent and Sapridom.

Note: For click-by-click video guidance, watch the **SilentMoves Video #15 Edit Products: overview section** at new.designWPsite.com/videos. It shows all the mouse clicks discussed above.

Now, for our main products display, there is no section left for us to repurpose or manipulate. We have to create a brand new section for our Products instead of editing what we already have. First, let's **delete all the sections** below the overview section. Choose each section by hovering in its content area and click on the 'x' on top of the section. Now we're ready to bring on our Products Section.

Creating a new section: Product displays

To get our Product Display section going, the Starter Templates plugin we installed comes to our rescue yet again. If we scroll down the Products page in the content pane, we see a blank space below the Overview section

Brief for the products page

- Our client wants his 9 products to be highlighted with photo and text

- In the masthead they want a background photo with a CTA button

- They want an overview section that talks about all the products in general with a reference photo that suggests Pharma

we just completed. The blank space carries three icons in the center of the page: a plus icon, a folder icon, and the Starter Templates icon.

Click the Starter Templates icon on the right. You'll be taken to a template library, featuring many pages and blocks. It's the blocks that we are after. Click on the 'Blocks' tab on top.

In the dropdown menu at the top left of the screen, choose Services among the various categories listed. I chose the first option on the page for our section by clicking on it. See the screenshot below.

A close-up view confirms that this choice is promising. There is an image on top with a title and a description in each of the four columns. That will suit us perfectly fine. Since we have 9 products to showcase, we can always make this a row of three instead of four and duplicate the row twice. All doable. Let's click on the blue 'Import block' button above.

You now get a close-up view of the chosen block. Once you're satisfied, click the blue button on the top right that reads 'Import Block.' This inserts the block onto the page.

We now delete the heading that reads 'Supporting Heading' by clicking in its top right corner and clicking the 'x' that appears. We change the text of 'Secondary Heading' to 'Products.' Left-align the heading by clicking the left-align icon under the Style tab of Elementor.

We hover the mouse above the image in the fourth column towards the **upper left of the column** (which shows the column icon of vertical lines, not the pencil icon on the right side which only deletes the image and not the column.) Click on the 'x' that appears.

So now we have 3 columns in place, ready to receive new images, new headlines and new descriptive text.

Start with the first column on the left. Follow our usual drill. Change the image with the one given in the download folder for this chapter. Remember to provide a Border Radius of 12 to curve the corners of the image. Change the headline and description using the pdf given to you. We know by now how to change images and text. This is nothing different or

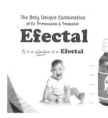

Apitone: The appetite stimulant

Apitone is an appetite stimulant with Cyproheptadine and Trichloine Citrate. A good appetite stimulant that increases fat emulsification, transport and utilisation.

Efectal: For diarrhoeal infection

For mixed diarrhoeal infection. Efectal Suspension is a unique combination of Co-Trimoxazole and Tinidazole for an effective solution. Comes in a 50 ml therapeutic pack.

Decolic: For colic pain and inflammation

Decolic tablets have Dicyclomine HCl (20 mg) and Paracetamol (500 mg) for relieving colic pain. It is a trusted combination with confirmed safety record and convenient dosage.

new. Now complete images two and three. Your work should end up looking like the screenshot above.

Click on UPDATE as ever to save your work. Watch the **SilentMoves Video #16 Display products on Products page** at <u>new.designWPsite.com/videos</u> to create this section.

Now that a row has been created, let's duplicate it. Hover over the row and right-click on the top 9-dot cluster. From the menu that appears, click on Duplicate. It instantly creates a second row. Do the same thing once again and create a third row as well. We are ready to replace the text and images in the second and third rows now, working column by column.

I'll spare you the tedious instructions. Just get on to the second row and replace the image in the first column with the one in the download folder for the chapter. Replace the headline and description with the ones I've given you in the pdf document. Move to the second column, rinse and repeat. Till you get to the last column of row three. You may let out a soft whistle now in relief. This kind of repetitive drudgery is something you have to get used to sometimes. It's part of the building process. Welcome to website creation!

If you mentally take a few steps back, what you've gone and done is basically finished the Products page. The masthead on top is in place. So is the Overview section below it with a royalty-free image downloaded from a website. And the display of 9 products with their images, titles and descriptions has been well laid out.

It's what you might call a productive day.

Chapter Summary

- You learned about the client's brief for the Products page

- You did an audit of the templates page to evaluate it
- You created the masthead section with a background image, headline, text and added a CTA button
- You repurposed the Overview section and learned to add a royalty-free image from a popular website
- You created a new Product display section by using a Starter Templates block template and modifying it to display 9 products
- You watched 3 SilentMoves videos: **#14 Edit masthead on Products page**, **Video #15 Edit Products: overview section** and **Video #16 Display products on Products page**

◆◆◆

7. Finalizing the Contact page

PREPARATION: Download the contactpage.zip file for use with this chapter.

T oday is when we do the Contact page in quick time and also clean up the main menu on top of every page. Make sure Local by Flywheel is running and you click on the WP Admin button to get into the backend of your site in the browser. Get to the front end and get on the Home page. Take a look at the main menu in the header.

Editing the Main Menu

Let's start with the menu clean-up. If you remember, we did a minor clean up earlier by changing the name of the menu item 'Company' to 'About'. We did that by going to the Company page (or the About page) and then using the 'Edit page' link in the admin bar to change the title of the page from Company to About. We also changed the URL in the right column to make it /about instead of /company.

You can refresh your memory if you wish by going to the end of Chapter 5 to see what we did then. It's not necessary, though. The point I'm making is that we edited the page title to change a menu item's name. But, generally speaking, changes to the menu are made elsewhere—and we'll learn about that now.

The main menu is in the header part of the website and as noted this does not come under the control of Elementor (free version.) We have to **go to Astra to make changes to anything in the header.**

Click on Customize in the admin bar. That takes us to the Astra back end. We've been here before. In the left column click on Header Builder. Then click on the Primary Menu option, followed by the Configure Primary Menu from here link. A list of Menus are displayed. We need the Primary Menu, so click on the Edit Menu link just below the Primary Menu dropdown (see screenshot below) to help us modify the individual menu items inside of the Primary Menu.

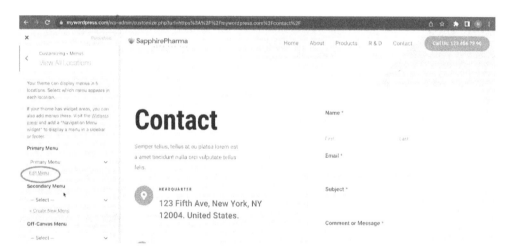

The menu items listed here are: Home, About, Products, R & D, and Contact. Which is exactly what is there on our main menu on every page. As a small example on how to edit the menu, click on the down arrow to the right of the About item in the Astra panel. In the Navigation Label box below, change 'About' to 'About us.' In the content panel, you'll see the instant change in the main menu on top.

Now open the R & D menu item by clicking on the down arrow next to it. We don't need a page like this on our site. So click on the red Remove link. The item vanishes from the menu. At a later stage, we will come back here once we have built the blog to add the 'Blog' item to the menu. For now, we're done here. Click on the blue Publish button on top of the Astra panel to save the work.

In the content panel, to the right of the main menu, there is a green button with a phone number in it. To alter the number, hover your mouse over the button and click on the pencil that appears. In the Astra panel, change the text to 'Fix appointment.' Click on the Publish button to save.

Note: For click-by-click video guidance, watch the **SilentMoves video #17 Edit Main Menu** at new.designWPsite.com/videos. It shows you all the mouse clicks discussed here.

Editing the Contact page

Already, the Contact page provided by our template looks all set to go. All the ingredients are there - a Contact title, intro text under it, an address, a mail id and phone number, and a contact form alongside. What's to complain?

Click on 'Edit with Elementor' in the top admin bar to get into edit mode for the page.

As practice, use the pdf download to change the intro text, address, phone number and email id using Elementor's panel as before.

In similar vein, scrolling down the page, change the person's image with that of the company director from the chapter download. Remember to make the Border Radius 12 to curve the corners of the image. Change the quote alongside with the text given as also the name and designation below the quote. All familiar stuff by now, right?

Note: For click-by-click video guidance, watch the **SilentMoves Video #18 Set up contact page** at <u>new.designWPsite.com/videos</u>. It shows all the mouse clicks so far.

All is good. Do you want to talk about the elephant in the room? It's the contact form! It's sitting pretty in plain sight, yet the **contact form can only be edited outside of Elementor**.

By 'edited' I mean adding a new field like 'Phone' or deleting an existing one like 'Subject.' Such things can be done only within a plugin called **WP Forms** and not directly on the page. And if you're wondering when we installed a plugin called WP Forms, you have to know it was done behind the scenes without your knowledge.

You see, when we installed our first plugin Starter Templates, it installed (as already noted) the Elementor plugin as well as the Astra theme for us. What it also did was quietly install another plugin called WP Forms (free version). This is a popular plugin to generate forms (like our contact form) for use on our site. So there.

If you think about it, such forms not only have to display fields like name, email, etc. but **they also have to do something**. When a visitor fills up the form and clicks on the Submit button, their details and message have to be mailed to you as the site owner.

The default mail that a visitor's message gets sent to is the **admin email of the site** which is something you decided when you set up WordPress > Settings > General page. Go to the backend of your site and click on **Settings > General** from the left, black column. You'll see your admin email there. That's the mail id to which our contact form will sent its messages.

Let's edit the contact form now.

Editing the Contact Form

Let's say you want to **delete the 'Subject' field**. Not many sites have a subject field these days. It's one less field for the visitor to fill up. That makes it more inviting for a prospect to send the form.

Where do you go to make this deletion? If you've made any changes on the page, remember to UPDATE before moving away from this page.

Get out of Elementor by clicking on the hamburger icon (3 lines) on the left of the band on top and then click 'Exit to Dashboard.' You'll be in the

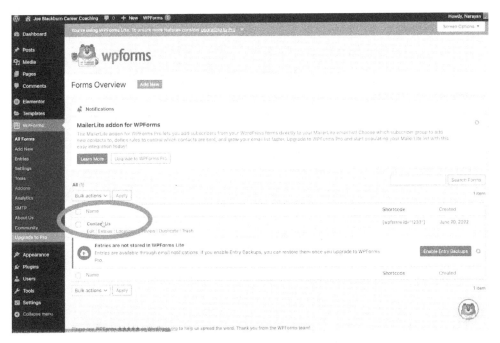

WordPress back end. From the left column, hover over the WP Forms menu item and click on 'All Forms' from the fly-out menu that appears.

On the page that now appears, crowded with copy, it's easy to miss the 'Contact us' form near the center of the page. See the screenshot above.

When you hover over it, a tiny menu appears underneath. Click on 'Edit' in the tiny menu. You will see the form fields big and upfront displayed on the next page. **Hover over the Subject field and click on the red delete bin that appears on the far right.** The field is gone.

Click on the name field and then click on the 'Click to edit' link that appears at bottom right. In the left column, under the Format dropdown, select the Simple option to have a single box for the name instead of First and Last Name boxes. Now click on the orange 'Save' button on the top right of the page.

The job is done. But for your information, it may be useful to know that if you click on the 'Settings' item in the far left vertical menu (underneath the cuddly bear logo) you will see 'Notifications' as a menu item in the new menu alongside. Click on 'Notifications.' Under Default Notification, you can change the Send To Email Address from {admin_email} to some other email of your choice. Remember to click the orange 'Save' button on top when you're done.

Note: For click-by-click video guidance, watch the **SilentMoves Video #19 Edit Contact Form** at new.designWPsite.com/videos. It shows all mouse clicks discussed above.

Get back to the front end and review your handiwork on the Contact page. The Contact page is all cleaned up with minimal fields for a visitor to fill in. **Fill in the form and send a message to yourself** to check it works properly.

Chapter Summary

· You edited the main menu items in the Astra back end

· You edited the text matter in the intro section as also the address, mail id, etc.

· You changed the image below and the quotation alongside

· You learned about WP Forms

· You edited the WP Forms contact form and deleted the 'Subject' field and modified the Name field

· You watched 3 SilentMoves videos: **Video #17** Edit Main Menu, **Video #18** See up Contact Page and **Video #19**: Edit Contact Form

◆ ◆ ◆

8. Creating a Blog (optional)

PREPARATION: To use the sample content for use with the Blog page, download the blogpage.zip file from here: <u>new.designWPsite.com/ downloads</u>

W ordPress started life as a blogging platform. If you want to include a blog on your website, it's easy enough as we'll see in this chapter. If you have no use for a blog, skip this chapter.

Strangely, a popular page builder like Elementor—the free version—has no features to offer us. There are no nicely designed pages to drag across or cool-looking blocks to bring over.

You need the paid version of Elementor to get all the extra blogging features including spiffy layouts. If yours is primarily or heavily a blogging site, you'll want to look into the paid Pro version of Elementor.

We will continue to use the free Elementor builder on our site, forgoing the bells and whistles. For normal sites that have blogs as well as other regular pages (as against solely being a blogging site), this should be nicely adequate.

To get our blog going, **we will use WordPress's page builder called Gutenberg**. Gutenberg comes with WordPress, so there's nothing new to install. It works similar to Elementor in that you can insert pre-made blocks (elements) into the layout.

What we call a blog is basically a collection of individual blog posts written over time, often by the same author. Copy the headline of the first blog post from the downloaded text for this chapter. We are going to create our first blog post. Ready?

Oh, wait... a little digression first

I want you to be aware of something that happens now and then when you're building a site on WordPress. That happened to me just now, so I'm raising it. It could have already happened to you or it may happen day after tomorrow.

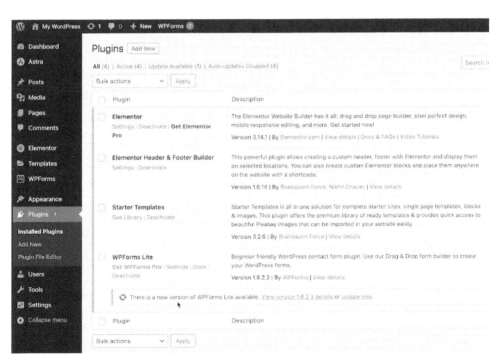

First, make sure that the Local by Flywheel app is running. Click on the website's name in the left column, click on the WP admin to get to the back end of our website. And here's the interesting thing I saw. See that round badge with the number 1 in it against Plugins (screenshot above)? Also, when I click on the Dashboard link on top of the black column I see the item Updates with a similar red badge.

When I click on Plugins, it's telling me that the WP Forms plugin has a new version available and I can update it now. Obviously, the exact screen shown above will not be the one that shows up for you. But **something similar will show up for some plugin (or theme) for you at some time or the other.** It's part of the WordPress ecosystem that themes and plugins (and even WordPress itself) keeps updating through the year. It's a good thing to keep your website updated with the latest versions.

So if such a thing happens to you and you see a red flag (as it will), here's what to do. I'll tell you what I did when I got the above screen and you can follow suit when your time comes.

I clicked the Dashboard link and clicked on Updates under it. You will see all updates listed here in a plugins group followed by a themes group. I selected the checkbox next to the plugins list to select all the plugins in the list. And clicked on the Update button. In my case, there was only one plugin to update and no themes. So WP Forms Lite got updated successfully in a few moments.

I went back to the WordPress updates page to make sure everything was up to date. The red badges had gone and we are now good to go.

Digression over.

Creating a blog post

Get to the backend of your site. **Click on Posts > Add New.** Paste the headline from the downloaded text (blog post #1) into the title box: *Reconciling Differences.* In the blank box below the title, copy-paste the subheading matter for the blog post: *Where the industry is heading with contrary opinions.*

Since we want the subheading to look like one and not like regular text, click on the Paragraph icon on the extreme left of the formatting bar that appears. See screenshot below. Choose Heading from the menu that appears. Since the size is too big, click on H2 and from the menu that appears select H4. That should do fine.

Click on the empty space in the next line below. And copy-paste the body text from the pdf here. Yup, the whole thing. As the number of blog posts grows over time, it is customary to **group posts into categories.** It is also good practice to start a blog with some categories in mind and start associating each post with a specific category.

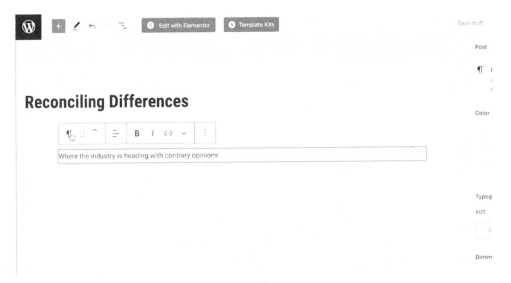

Let's assign a category to this first post we've just created. If you want to take your blog seriously and build it over time, organizing individual blog posts into categories is a must.

In the right column, make sure you are in the Post tab and not the Block tab (found at the top of the column.) As you scroll down, you will see 'Categories' (which you may have to click on to open the section if it isn't already open.) You will see a single category listed there called 'Uncategorized.' Enjoy the irony. Click on 'Add New Category' link and type in 'Pharma News' to signify this post is about that.

Don't worry that the actual copy has nothing to do with anything remotely pharmaceutical. Consider it placeholder text.

To add the category, click on the 'Add New Category' button below. This will add the category to your blog (and also place a tick mark beside it to assign it to this post) and this category option will be available to every post you create from now on.

Blog posts also generally have a **main image or a lead image** that goes with them.

WordPress calls it a **'featured image.'** If you scroll down the right column a bit more, you'll find a grey box with the words 'Set featured image.' Click on it.

You'll be taken to the Media Library which you have visited a few times before. Select the efectal.jpg image that is already in the library. Click on the 'Set featured image' button at the bottom right to bring it into your blog post.

We now have everything that we want in our post – the main heading or title, a subheading, main text, a chosen category, and a featured image.

It's time to **publish the post.** Click on the blue 'Publish' button on the top right of the page. You'll have to click on it twice. At the bottom you will see a black band with a 'View Page' link. Click on it to go to the front end and see the blog post.

The post looks cool. But there is a blank area to the right. It would be nice to have a sidebar there. Click on 'Customize' in the admin bar on top of the page to get into the Astra back end. Click on the Sidebar link. In the Default Layout section, select the Right Sidebar option, the third one. Click the blue Publish button on top. Click on the 'x' to the top left to get out of the Customizer. There, the post looks neater, right?

Take a closer look at the sidebar and you'll see that the widgets repeat for some reason. To delete the extra set of widgets, watch the **SilentMoves Video #20 Create Blog Post** at <u>new.designWPsite.com/videos</u> to guide you on all the moves, including how to delete the extra widgets.

What you see on the front end has the featured image prominently at the top with the title below it. Below the title is the 'meta' information – category, author name, and the date. The full text should follow below it. See screenshot above. Notice the right column with its useful items including a search box on top. Scroll down the page to get a full idea of how the blog post has turned out.

Cool? Now it's your turn.

Using the same techniques, **create the remaining 5 blog posts using the downloaded text for this chapter**. Assign two more posts to the category of 'Pharma News' and the remaining three posts to a new category called 'Drug info.' Use the visuals suggested by the pdf download for each post. They are visuals you already have in the Media Library, so there's nothing new to get.

You must create this handful of blog posts. You need **a set of blog posts in place to create a 'Blog' page on your site** which will feature excerpts from your recent posts with thumbnail-sized featured images.

When you're done creating the blog posts, go to the WordPress back end and click on Posts > All Posts in the left column. This page lists all the blog posts you've created. There should be six of them in total with three of them in the 'Pharma News' category and the other three in the 'Drug info' category.

So get to work and copy-paste the additional blog posts before getting to create the blog page as explained below.

Creating the Blog page

To create a Blog page that contains excerpts from your latest blog posts, WordPress requires us to **create a new blank page** (not a post.)

You can title this blank page anything you like: Our Pharma Advice, Latest from the Pharma World, Expert Comments, and so on. We will title this page simply 'SapphireBlog.'

Remember, we are not creating a post. We are creating a **page** that will hold all our post excerpts. That's the way WordPress rolls. And it's been doing it for decades.

Once ready, this page will display a listing of brief excerpts of your blog posts, appearing in reverse chronological order. Which is a fancy way of saying the more recent posts show up first and older posts show up later.

We then link this blog page to an item called 'SapphireBlog' in the main menu. Visitors click on that, get on to the blog page, review the excerpts and click on any of them to explore a specific blog post in its entirety.

Let's **create the Blog page** then. Go to the backend of your site and click on Pages > Add New from the left column. In the title box, type 'SapphireBlog'. That's it.

Don't do anything else. Save it by clicking on the blue 'Publish' button on the top right twice. You're done.

What? How does this work? There's nothing on the page! How will it display the blog excerpts? WordPress works in mysterious ways. What

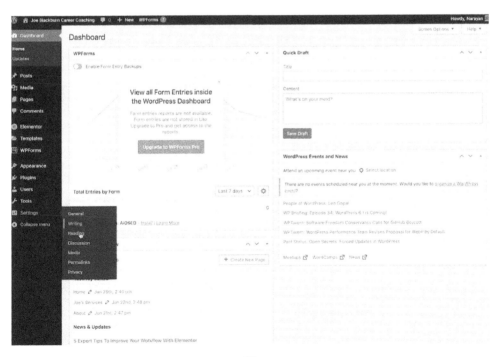

you're about to do in the next step below turns this blank page into a page like no other. It truly becomes our Blog page.

Here's the magical next step (see screenshot above.) Go to the backend and **click on Settings > Reading.** Against 'Homepage' notice that the page 'Home' has been chosen. But against the 'Posts page' nothing has been chosen. Click on the dropdown menu and select 'SapphireBlog' which is our designated page for 'holding' blog posts.

Click on the blue 'Save Changes' button at the bottom. Now click on **Pages > All Pages** in the left column. You will see all the pages your site contains.

Note: For click-by-click video guidance, watch the **SilentMoves Video #21 Create a Blog Page** at <u>designWPsite.com/videos</u>. It shows you how to create the Blog page.

You will see the page 'SapphireBlog' in the All Pages listing. Hover over it and see a sub-menu appear beneath. Click on 'View' to see the main blog page on the front end. And—voila!—this empty blog page is no longer empty. It is anything but. **All the excerpts are there from each of the 6 blog posts you created.**

Note: You can see the **finished version of the Blog page** at new.designWPsite.com/sapphireblog. Compare it with your own blog page. Close enough?

A neat little column on the right displays the recent posts as a list of titles. Your visitor can click on any of these titles and be taken to the relevant blog article in depth. If you see a blank right column, see the help video to get it working for you.

Now that the Blog page is ready, let us **link this page to a menu item on the Main Menu** at the top of every page. Click on the site name on the far left of the black, admin band on top. From the dropdown menu that appears, click on 'Menus.' You'll be taken to the Menus Edit page.

Make sure you're seeing the Primary Menu items and not some other menu. Watch the help video to get sorted on this. In the left column look for the SapphireBlog page. If you can't see it there, click on the next tab that reads 'View All.'

Click on the checkbox next to Blog to tick it. Click on the 'Add to Menu' button below to add it. Watch it appear in the listing of menu items on the right part of the page. You can grab the SapphireBlog box with your mouse and drag it a couple of places above, just below Home. Click on the 'Save Menu' button at the bottom right.

Get back to the front end. And you should see the main menu now featuring the SapphireBlog item as well. Click on it. And you should be on your SapphireBlog page. Click on any title. And you should be taken to that blog post. The blog feature on your website is now in place. You are really good at this. Congratulations!

Chapter Summary

- You used Gutenberg to create your blog posts
- You learned how to assign a category to blog posts
- You uploaded a featured image to go with your blog posts
- You created 6 blog posts in all
- You learned how to create a Blog page and made it display your blog post excerpts
- You added a 'SapphireBlog' menu item and linked it to the Blog page
- You watched the comprehensive **SilentMoves Video #20** Create Blog Posts and **Video #21** Create a Blog page

◆ ◆ ◆

9. Editing the Home page

PREPARATION: To use the sample content for use with the Home page, download the homepage.zip file from here: <u>new.designWPsite.com/downloads</u>

I think it's a great idea to build the Home page last. Once you know what goes into the other pages and what they look like, it becomes easier to build the Home page.

Think of the **home page as a content sampler to the various pages** within the site while also serving up the main benefits of doing business with you.

Note: To look at the **finished version of our home page** on your site, visit: new.designWPsite.com/home. This is the filled-in content and look we are aiming for.

The brief for the Home page

Our imaginary client told us that they want **seven sections** on the page.

The brief for the Home page

- The client wants a masthead with a background image, brand promise and CTA button

- They want a counter to display the key metrics

- They want a legacy section to briefly showcase their founder and past expertise

- A values section highlighting the 3 pillars of trust

- Key strengths and a paragraph on customer trust

- They want a testimonial section from doctors

- Their famous three brands highlighted

Let's consider the first three requirements as a group and get them done first: the **masthead**, the **counter** and the **legacy** sections. As before, they want the masthead on this page too to contain a background image, a headline and a CTA button. Let's begin with that.

Editing the Masthead section

From the home page on the front end, click on the 'Edit with Elementor' link in the admin bar above. (Of course, you've already made sure that Local by Flywheel is running in the background.) Take a moment to audit the template's ready-made home page. The masthead is there ready for our usual edits to get in shape. Not much of a challenge here, really.

There is a counter in place just below the masthead. How convenient is that! We have to change the metrics and we're good to go.

And the section below this can easily be the legacy section with copy in the right column and the founder's photo on the left.

On with our masthead edit. Hover the mouse over the masthead section and once the pink border around the section appears, click on the middle icon (with the 9 dots) at the top of the border.

In the Elementor panel on the left (it should say 'Edit Section' or 'Edit Container' on top depending on your Elementor version), click on the 'Style' tab on top and then the tiny image below. From the Media Library choose the image I've given you for this section by uploading it: **masthead-home.jpg** and click the 'Insert Media' button.

It is useful to know how to tweak this image if it doesn't cover the full area of the section or is otherwise wonky. **Under the various settings under the image in the Elementor column, you will find 'Size' which is by default set to 'Cover.'**

Almost all of the time, this setting of Cover will serve your needs best, but occasionally a setting like 'Contain' or 'Auto' may be perfect for a particular situation depending on the image you upload and its dimensions. Experiment. In all likelihood, 'Cover' should do the job.

Also the setting for Position should generally be 'Center Center.' The Repeat setting should be 'No-repeat.' Click on the UPDATE button below to save the changes.

We once again notice that the background image is 'bleeding' onto the header area above, making the menu items unreadable. We know the solution for we've seen this situation before. Click on the Advanced tab on top, unlink the values for the Margin setting by clicking on the link icon in the far right and enter 100 in the Top box. That will push down the masthead section by 100 pixels and steer clear of the header area.

To change the headline and the description text below it, you already know the drill. Click into them, one after the other, and make the changes in the Elementor column. Use the copy matter from the pdf that you downloaded for this chapter.

The pdf also gives you the copy for the tiny subheading above the main headline. Get that in place too.

Click on the button that reads 'Learn More.' In the Elementor panel change the Text to 'Know More' and link it to the About page.

Note: For click-by-click video guidance, watch the **SilentMoves Video #22 Edit home page sections I** at <u>new.designWPsite.com/videos</u>. It shows all mouse clicks discussed above to complete the masthead section.

Although our first section is done, when we look at it, the body text is not very readable against the background. We can change the colour of it by selecting it and in the Edit Text Editor panel, click on the Style tab. and against Text Color click on the tiny globe icon and choose one of the white shades. Theme Color 6 worked fine for me. You can UPDATE and that certainly feels better.

Editing the Counter section

We can get on with the next section which is the counter ticker bars or the counter section. Use the pdf for this chapter as a guide to get the correct numbers we have to input. For instance, we are talking about 60 products, not 320 as the template says. Select the number in the Elementor panel (it now reads Edit Counter on top) enter 60 in the Ending Number box.

In a similar way, fill in 71 instead of 128. And 2k employees instead of 12k and 500 doctors instead of 24 countries. For the last one, you also have to click on the word 'countries' and change it to 'doctors' in the Elementor panel. Also, instead of '71 patents' it should be '71 cities.'

OK, so we are done with the counter section. We are steaming head, it appears. Yet again, watch the SilentMoves video if you're in any doubt on how to go about this.

Click on the pink UPDATE button to save your work. Go to the front end to check your handiwork on the page thus far.

Creating the Legacy section

We need the legacy section below the counter. As noted, the current section in the template (see screenshot below) pretty much has all the elements our brief demands. Let's begin with the image of the founder in

the left column which will replace the lady there right now. Click on her image and then click on the thumbnail image in the Elementor panel.

We have used the founder's image before in the About page. So it's already there in your Media Library (founder.jpg.) Use that image now to fill in the left column in the content panel. Remember to do the styling of the border radius of 12 as usual.

Regarding the size of the image itself, it does feel a little too big. In the Style tab of Edit Image in the Elementor panel, we can change the width to whatever it is that we want. 80% instead of the entire 100% worked for me just fine.

Now it's a question of changing all the text elements in the right column one by one: the green subheading, headline, body text, quotation and the name and designation of the Director. We've done copy edits like these quite a few times before. Use your knowledge to get these elements done with the help of the text I have provided you in the pdf for this chapter. The finished Legacy section should look like the screenshot shown below. Once done, you can get out of Elementor to take a look at the front end of the Home page. The top three sections are done. And looking

good! Use the help video **SilentMoves Video #22 Edit home page sections I** at new.designWPsite.com/videos.

Editing the Values section

Let's take the remaining four sections we need for the home page as a group of things to be done. And let's knock them off one by one.

The brief for the Home page

- The client wants a masthead with a background image, brand promise and CTA button

- They want a counter to display the key metrics

- They want a legacy section to briefly showcase their founder and past expertise

- A values section highlighting the 3 pillars of trust

- Key strengths and a paragraph on customer trust

- They want a testimonial section from doctors

- Their famous three brands highlighted

The Values section, as is clear from the pdf download, requires us to talk about the company's 3 pillars of trust. It gives us a headline that pretty much states their corporate philosophy. And there are three blocks of copy, each representing a 'pillar.'

With these in mind, if we look at the actual template in front of us, we have the headline element followed by six blocks of text in two rows. See screenshot below. Of course, we don't need six blocks, we need just three. So we can delete the bottom row of three blocks.

Congue ultric in pellentesque sodales egestas faucibus accumsan.

Innovation	Teamwork	Sustainable
Id leo massa lacinia morbi pulvinar venenatis, etiam amet purus in interdum proin nisl morbi eleifend	Senectus nisl ultricies mi urna, curabitur amet adipiscing eget convallis ultricies lacus eget sed adipiscing eu	Sed morbi ut ullamcorper sodales et congue laoreet massa sit sit hendrerit morbi gravida malesuada sem
Integrity	Excellence	Commitment

Get into the Edit with Elementor mode (if you aren't in that mode already). Hover over the second row of text boxes till you see a pink border enclosing ONLY the three boxes in the bottom row. Click on the 'x' at the top of the border to delete this inner section.

Click on the main headline. Go to the pdf download for the chapter and copy the main headline (in the Values section.) Replace the existing headline in the usual way using the Elementor panel on the left.

Complete each of the three blocks one by one by replacing the smaller headlines and text with the ones from the pdf.

We keep the copy in the left column that reads 'Our values' the way it is because that happens to match the text in our pdf. With that, we've got the Values section done without breaking into a sweat. Remember to click the UPDATE button and review your work on the front end.

The 3 pillars of building Trust

Research	Collaboration	Integrity
Research is the cornerstone for innovation. We stay ahead by making sure that we have already found solutions before you seek them.	It's not just about building teamwork within the company, but also about going beyond to work along with world experts as well as understanding patients.	We insist on transparency across all levels of interactions and also unfailingly keep our commitment of quality and delivery to ensure absolute dependability and accountability.

Your finished section should look like the one above.

Creating the Key Strengths section

The next section is about the firm's key strengths. If you check the pdf download, what they require is a bullet list of points. Each point is a subheading with a line of text below explaining the main point. There are 4 points in total: clinical development, regulatory access, biotech, and reach & distribution.

Except for the last point, the others are there already in the pharma template. The explanatory line of text under each point can easily be edited with the new copy from the pdf. All good so far. But the client also wanted these 4 points to be featured in the left column where an image currently is. In the right column they wanted a subheading, a main headline and sub-text.

These three elements are already there on top of the right column. So we'll leave them there and move all the points below to the left column after deleting the image there.

So get into 'Edit with Elementor' mode. Hover on the image and right click on the pencil icon at the top left and delete it by clicking on the 'x' that's right there when the pencil icon opens out.

With the image gone and the left column empty, let's get the bullet points over from the right to the left column. Hover your mouse over the first bullet point and grab the pencil icon in the top right corner. Dragging it drags the entire bullet text box. Drag it and drop it in the left column.

Similarly, move over the rest of the bullet points to the left column, one under the other. Now we have to change the text under the main bullet points as also the fourth bullet point itself.

Remember to watch the **SilentMoves Video #23 Edit home page sections II** to help you with this part of the home page build.

Click on the first bullet point. In the Elementor panel, the line on top says, 'Edit Icon Box.' This is a new element or widget we haven't used before. It is similar to the Image Box we used. The Icon Box is a composite element of an icon, a title and a description, similar to the Image Box which had an image instead of an icon.

We can copy over the text from the pdf for the line of text under the first point, 'Clinical Development' and paste it in the Description box. The Title is already filled in and that's fine.

In the Icon box above the Title, notice the icon of a microscope. Clicking on it takes you a library of icons from which you can select whichever you want. You can click on it to see the library, but we don't need to change it because this one serves our purpose well.

In similar fashion, copy over the lines of text for the second and third Icon Boxes and leave their current icons the way they are. Click on the fourth and final Icon Box. Change the Title to 'Reach and Distribution.' Change the line of text to what's given in the pdf download.

Here, we can change the icon to something more relevant. Click on the icon in the Elementor panel to get to the icon library. In the search box,

type in 'truck.' See the screenshot. Click on a truck image and click on the Insert button at bottom right. The icon now shows up in the Elementor panel as well as in the content panel.

Click the UPDATE button to save the work. And the left column of bullet points is complete.

To finish this section, let's complete the work for the right column of text. Using the pdf download, replace the headline with the given headline as well as the text below. This should be an easy task by now. Remember to save your work with the pink UPDATE button. The completed Key Strengths section will look as above in the screenshot.

When you look at the template and observe what's there below the Key Strengths section, we see a 'purpose section.' We have no need for this. Hover your mouse over this section (while in Edit with Elementor mode) and click on the 'x' at the top of the pink border surrounding the whole section. That will delete the section. Great.

According to our brief, we need the Testimonials section next followed by our Brands section to finish off the Home page. The end is in sight!

However, the template we have in front of us has no Testimonials section for us to repurpose. But it does have a Brands section just below the Key Strengths section. Let's adapt to the situation then.

We'll get the Brands section done right away because there's one staring us in the face. And we'll worry about the Testimonials section once we finish this one. OK?

Editing the Brands section

Our brief wants us to highlight the firm's 3 famous brands. We have the jpg images of these already so we don't have to download anything new. What we notice in the template is that there is a common subheading on top of the section that reads 'Our Brands' followed by 5 columns with a logo in each.

All we need is 3 columns with possibly a 4th column to display a button that reads "See all" with a link to the Products page. We will not use the 5th column. Toward deleting this, hover your mouse on the 5th column (while in 'Edit with Elementor' mode) over the pencil icon in the top right corner. This brings up the 'x' you can click to delete the image (logo) there but keep the column space intact.

If you had clicked the column icon on the *left* top corner instead of the pencil icon, you'd find an 'x' to delete the column itself, not just the logo inside. The first 4 columns will then expand to fill the space caused by the deletion. Try it if you want. You can always press Cmd or Ctrl Z to undo it afterward.

By clicking on the 'x' on the pencil corner, you delete the logo but keep the space. Understanding this distinction will help you manage empty spaces they way you want.

Let's replace the logos with our product images. Click the first image in the first column. In the Elementor panel, click on the thumbnail and select the product Sapridom in the Media Library and insert it on our page the usual way. The pdf for the chapter wants us to similarly insert two more product images: Apitone and Efectal.

Remember to go to the Style tab for each image and adjust the Border Radius to 12 for getting the curved corners. Let's save the work by clicking the pink UPDATE button.

We need a button in the 4th column. Drag the Button widget from the Elementor pane as before and drop it in the 4th column. (Remember, to see the widgets, you have to click the cluster of dots to the right of the black band on top of the Elementor panel.) Change the default button text from 'Click here' to 'See all.'

To make the button useful, you can type in '/products' in the Link box. That's the page which has all the products of the company. To properly

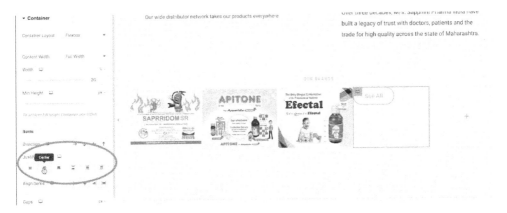

align the button vertically, go to the Style tab by selecting the 4th column icon (not the image pencil icon.)

In the Elementor panel, the heading should now read, 'Edit Container' and not 'Edit Button.' There in the Justify setting choose the 'center' icon as shown in the screenshot above. And in the next setting of Align Items select the center icon again. The button will now be centred correctly vis-a-vis the product images on its left. Check the help video to be sure.

Click on the UPDATE button. We are done with our brands for the most part. You can look at the green subheading on top and revise it to read 'Our famous brands' by clicking on the subheading and changing the Title in

the Edit Heading panel. Also click the left-align button in the Alignment setting at the bottom of the Elementor panel. UPDATE one final time - to get this section in place.

Creating the Testimonials section

The final section left to do on the Home page is the Testimonial section according to the client brief. When you scroll down the page we've been working on thus far, we've come a long way, starting with the masthead and ending with the Brands section.

As is evident, there is no section under the Brands section for us to edit (barring the 4-part footer section, of course.) So we have to create a brand new section from scratch to house our testimonials. A look at the pdf for the chapter tells us there are 3 testimonials from doctors we have to provide for. Once done, the end of the Home page is nigh!

Get into the 'Edit with Elementor' mode, if you aren't in that already. Below the Brands section, you'll see 3 icons (or maybe 4), the rightmost of which is the Starter Templates icon. Click on it to get into a page full of ready-made templates. Click on the Blocks tab on top of the page to see templates for sections (blocks) rather than for whole pages.

In the dropdown menu on the left, select 'Testimonials' to filter only templates for those. Toward the bottom of the page, I found a template that was perfect for our use with all the elements we want: a headline, interesting quote graphics, the testimonial text, name, designation and a small photograph as well. And the design was meant for 3 testimonials, no more, no less. See screenshot below. Click on it to see the close-up view and click on Import Block button to get it onto our page.

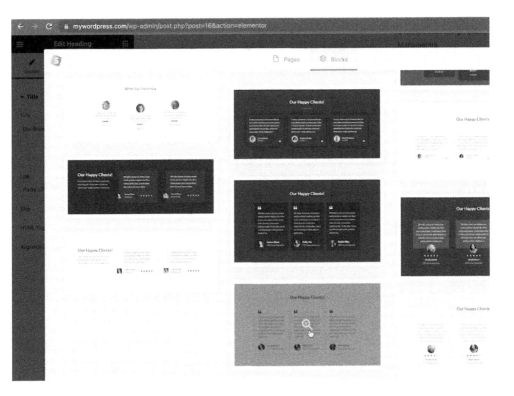

Before we do anything else, hover your mouse over the Brands section, grab it by the 9-dot 'select icon' on top and move the whole section downward. Place it after the Testimonial section and let go. That puts the page in correct order as per the client's requirements.

We notice that the subheading 'Our famous brands' on top of the Brands section is too close to the border above it. We hover our mouse over the Brands section and select it by clicking the 9-dot cluster on top of the pink border box. In the Elementor panel, we click on the Advanced tab on top and fill in 60 in the Top Margin box (without changing other values.) The subheading now has breathing space on top. Click on UPDATE to save your work.

Let's change the headline for the section that reads, 'Our happy clients' to the one in the pdf download for the chapter. Also choose the left-align icon in the Elementor panel to make the headline follow the consistency of the entire page layout. (You can also left-align the small divider line underneath the headline to keep it all well ordered.)

Now click on the main text of the first testimonial and replace it with the text in the pdf. Nothing new here. Similarly, move over to the next two columns in turn and change the content of the text boxes there to match the copy in the pdf. If you click on the person's name at the bottom of the first column, you realise it's an Image Box that we've seen before. It's basically a composite widget with an image, a title and description grouped together.

The Elementor panel therefore reads Edit Image Box on top. File in the person's name in the Title box and their designation in the Description box. Click on the Image box in the Elementor panel and use the image from the pdf for the first testimonial. UPDATE.

In similar fashion, complete the two other Image Boxes in the second and third columns with information from the pdf for the chapter.

Once you UPDATE, not only the Testimonials section, but the whole of our Home page is done and dusted. You have marched from strength to strength.

Note: For click-by-click video guidance, watch the **SilentMoves Video #23 Edit home page sections II** at <u>new.designWPsite.com/videos</u>. It shows you how to complete the final 4 sections of the home page.

Get out of Elementor and go to the front end. Scroll down to see this section as a visitor would. You deserve some serious congratulations for sticking on and getting this done. You also deserve a break.

Chapter Summary

- You edited the masthead section with a new background image, headline, text and button
  - You edited the counter and legacy sections
  - You edited the values section
  - You edited the key strengths section
  - You deleted unwanted sections
  - You brought in a new Testimonial section with Starter Templates
  - You edited the Brands section with custom text and a button
  - You watched the SilentMoves **Videos #22 and #23**
  - You finished the basic website for the pharmaceutical firm!

◆ ◆ ◆

10. Must-have skills to learn

PREPARATION: To use the sample content for use with this chapter, download the skills.zip file from here: new.designWPsite.com/downloads

Let's start with learning how to **optimize images**. What exactly does this mean and why optimize images at all? A typical website has a lot of images in it. The website we just completed is no exception. Yet, nowhere along the way, we talked of optimizing images. How come?

It's because I gave you all the images that were already optimized. You didn't have to bother. When it comes to building your own site for your business, as you'd be doing shortly, there won't be a Narayan around to hand you pre-optimized images. Time to learn the skill, folks.

Optimizing images on your site

The bigger the image, the greater its resolution and the better it looks. But it comes at a cost - every hi-res image file is close to 1 MB if not more. That is simply too huge a size for web use.

Every image bank out there like pexels.com, unsplash.com, shutterstock.com, etc.—there are hundreds of them—will give you hi-res images each of which can be anywhere between 1 MB and 25 MB. Even your phone camera produces pretty large images.

By website standards, these are huge files to store in a database and serve to every visitor who comes calling at your site.

If the images on your website are ridiculously high in file-size, the pages will take forever to load. On the other hand, smaller file-size images make for a smooth and fast website.

Optimizing an image means reducing its size while maintaining decent quality. And size can mean one of two things:

Dimensions: An image that is 600 x 400 px (width by height measured in pixels) is preferable to an image that is 4800 x 3200 px for web usage.

File size: An image that is 250 kB is preferable to an image that is 3 MB (file size measured in kB or Mb.)

Before you upload an image to the Media Library it is good to get into the habit of noting its dimensions and file size.

To make an image ideal for web use, you have to **reduce its dimensions** to an optimal size, depending on how big you need it on the page. You also have to **reduce its file size** using a process known as **'compressing.'**

Once you've done both, you have optimized an image for web use. It's a crucial part of site building. It's easy to learn this skill with a few online resources to help you.

Let's take the image download for this chapter. The file imageopt.jpg is a horizontal image with dimensions of 5472 px by 3648 px and a file-size of 5.6 MB. That's real big by web standards.

As always, you have a SilentMoves video to guide you through the process once you get the hang of it here. Watch the **SilentMoves Video #024 Optimize images** at <u>new.designWPsite.com/videos</u>. It shows you how to optimize images for use on your website.

You know by now that all the numbers of imageopt.jpg are way above optimal. Consider the width of a normal computer screen. It is something around 1300 px perhaps. An image whose width is 5000 px is certainly overkill even if it was meant to occupy the full width of the screen.

And the file size of 5.6 MB is way over the limit for a single image. Let's get to work. (It's not that WordPress won't let you upload such heavy images. It will. But the price you pay in terms of page speed will be unacceptably high.)

Go over to **iloveimg.com** which is one of many such sites that can get the job done for us. I like its simplicity of use. Click on 'Resize Image' link in the main menu or in the display below the menu.

Grab our humongous image from your computer and drop it here. Or click on the blue button that reads 'Select Images' and upload it.

You'll see some resize options in the right column. The image file's original dimensions are filled in already. Reduce the width from 5472 px to 750 px. Note that the height also proportionately reduces to 500 px (keep the box 'Maintain aspect ratio' below checked.)

You've given your instructions for a size reduction and it's the software's turn to obey you and get it done. Click the blue 'Resize Images' button below.

The resized image should **auto-download** now. The reduction in dimensions is now done. (A happy side-effect of this reduction process is that the reduced dimensions automatically made the file-size too smaller. It is now 147 kB from its original 5.6 MB. But we can do better.) Now, onto compressing the image next.

For this, I prefer a site called **tinyjpg.com**. Its service is free up to a maximum of 20 images per day (at the time of writing.) It's totally easy to use.

Just drag our image (with the reduced dimensions) into the box on top of the home page at tinyjpg.com. The compression is done in a few seconds. While the dimensions are maintained at 750 x 500 px, the file size has magically gone down to 48 kB from 147 kB. Click on the download link alongside to get your hands on the compressed image and you're done.

Your image is now reduced in dimensions and also compressed. The optimization is done.

Read that again. It's 48 kB, not MB. Such an image will load fast!

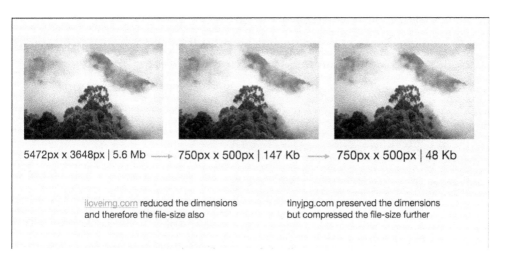

5472px x 3648px | 5.6 Mb ⟶ 750px x 500px | 147 Kb ⟶ 750px x 500px | 48 Kb

iloveimg.com reduced the dimensions
and therefore the file-size also

tinyjpg.com preserved the dimensions
but compressed the file-size further

While there are **plugins** to get automatic re-sizing and compression done, their effects are sometimes unreliable. I find that a few moments of dragging and dropping images in small batches on these two sites give great results.

And you don't have to think of them again, once they are optimized and uploaded to your site's Media Library.

As a thumb rule for what file size works best, **consider 250 Kb as the number to remember for full-width images.** Don't let any image go over that and it often should be much below that. For images that take up lesser screen width, anything in the 50 kB to 100 kB should be fine.

You will also develop a sensibility over a few weeks on what sizes work well on different parts of a page. This is invaluable expertise.

So am I saying that every image that you use on your website should be optimized first before uploading? Yes. Yes. And, before I forget, yes.

Setting up the site's favicon

Let's figure out how to set up our site's favicon now.

A favicon is a tiny graphic that shows up in the tab of a browser. In Chrome, for example, the favicon for YouTube shows up in the tab as in the screenshot alongside.

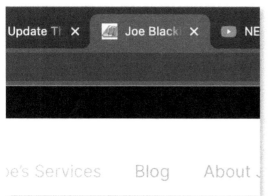

A favicon's job is to tell you which site is where at a glance when you have multiple browser tabs open. It's the kind of detail that goes toward making our fledgling site look professional. Editing or creating a favicon comes under the Astra theme rather than Elementor.

For this exercise, you can use the site icon I have given as part of your content download for this chapter. Or you can create a simple graphic that represents your site. It can even be the starting alphabet of your site name in an interesting and bold font style.

You can use a free online program like Canva to create your favicon. Since the final display is going to be small, **keep the design extremely simple**. Keep the size of the icon to 500 x 500 px.

Let's get to the Astra edit page. Click on the 'Customize' link on the admin bar on top of any page that you are on.

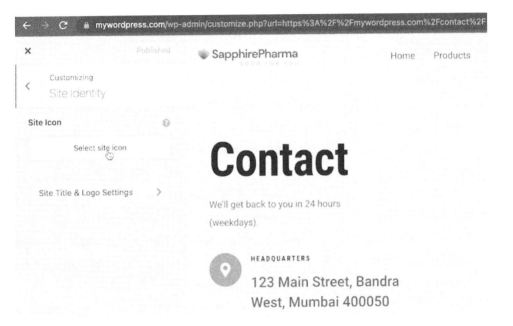

In the left column, click on 'Header Builder' and then on the 'Site Identity' link down the column. Then click on 'Select site icon' box that is above the Site Title & Logo Settings box (we've been here earlier.) See screenshot above.

In the Media Library select the favicon image you downloaded for this chapter (the file is favicon.png.) Click on the blue 'Select' button at the bottom right. Click on the 'Publish' button on top of the left column and you're done.

Exit the Astra edit page and look at the tab of your site. It should carry the icon you just inserted. Watch the **SilentMoves Video #25 Add a favicon** at new.designWPsite.com/videos. It shows you how to create a favicon for your site.

Inserting a video

We have no video displays of any kind on our site. What if you want to show a video on a page to illustrate a point you're making? This could be a video by a celebrity in your field or created by you.

If you want to display your own video(s) on your site, make note of the following point.

Unlike images, which you upload to the Media Library, **you don't upload video files to your own website**. Video files are huge and take up a lot of space. Your cheap hosting plan will probably not have enough resources to store and stream videos without a glitch, especially when many visitors land on your website simultaneously.

Besides, with sites like YouTube and Vimeo doing the dedicated business of hosting videos, you are better off uploading your videos there. **So if you're going the route of making your own videos, host them (for free) on YouTube.**

All you then need to figure out is how to link such videos uploaded on YouTube to your website. Linked properly, a preview of your video will show up on your site. When a visitor clicks on the play button, the video plays right there on your site, although in reality, it is YouTube that is streaming it.

If you're using someone else's videos to illustrate your points, it's the same procedure. Get the video link from YouTube and paste it into your page to make it show up there (we'll see in a moment how to do that.)

Note: Unlike images, you don't have to worry about copyright or permission to display a YouTube video (at least the ones that are freely available on their site, not the private or unlisted ones). People upload public videos on YouTube to get more exposure. By linking, your site is doing them a favor by giving them that extra exposure.

Danza Castellana by Torroba | DuJu

So how do we get a YouTube video to play on your site? Let's say you want to link to a specific video on YouTube from one of your blog posts. (The method is the same whether it's a blog post or any other page of your site.)

The first step is to go to the desired video page on YouTube. Copy the address of the page from the address bar on top. It will be in the form of "https://www.youtube.com/watch?v=stringofcharacters." This is the video link we need. See the screenshot above.

Back to your site. From the main blog page, reached by clicking 'Blog' on the main menu, click on any blog headline from the posts featured there. You'll be taken to that blog post in its entirety.

Click on the 'Edit post' link at top of the page (not the 'Edit with Elementor' link) which takes us to the WordPress back end of that post. Click at the end of any paragraph and press Enter or Return to create a new empty line where you want to insert the video.

Click on the '+' button at the right within the blue border and type in 'video' in the search box. The YouTube block will show up. See screenshot below. Select it and in the URL box paste the video link you saved. Click on the blue 'Embed' button to the right.

The video preview will spurt to life right there. Click on the blue 'Update' button on the top right of the page to save this new setting. Go to the front end of the blog post to check. Your video is now ready and in

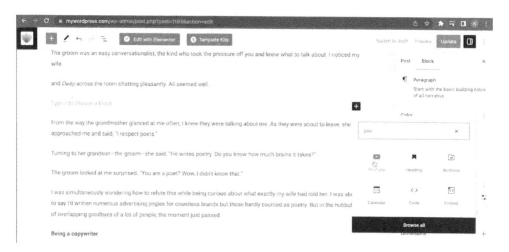

place, for all the world to see.

For click-by-click video guidance, watch the **SilentMoves Video #26 Insert video in a post** at <u>new.designWPsite.com/videos</u>. It shows you how to display a video in your blog post.

Creating a Privacy Policy page

Of all the so-called legal pages many websites tend to have, the very minimum is the Privacy Policy page.

Even if you don't do e-commerce or anything complex on your site, a Privacy Policy page is necessary, and legally required in many countries. If your site has a basic contact form and/or comments turned on for its blog (both true in our case), you are collecting user data, whether you think of it that way or not.

Someone is giving your their name and email at the very least and possibly a comment or two for your blog.

The issue is what you are, or your site is, planning to do with this user data. Why are you asking for it? What do you intend to do with it? What if a user asks you to remove all their data from your site? How would you respond to that?

And so forth. Your Privacy Policy page sets out, in concrete terms, the answers to concerns like these.

Since I'm not a lawyer, I'm not qualified to give you advice on what exactly you should or should not include on your Privacy Policy page. Google to your rescue! (Ask your lawyer to vet it if you want to be extra careful.)

I have found the site **https://termly.io** useful and easy to use. You answer a series of questions that pertain to your website and by the end of it, it gives you the text which you can copy-paste onto your website.

Where exactly do you paste this on your website? **On a new page that you create specifically for this purpose.** Let's do it.

Go to the back end and click on Pages > Add New. Enter the title text as 'Privacy Policy' and paste the copy you have created or been recommended in the text area. Click the 'Publish' button. You're done.

The link to this page is generally placed in the footer so that it is 'reachable' from every page of your site. From the front end, click on 'Customize' to get to the Astra back end.

(Remember, the header and footer details are not managed with Elementor but with Astra.)

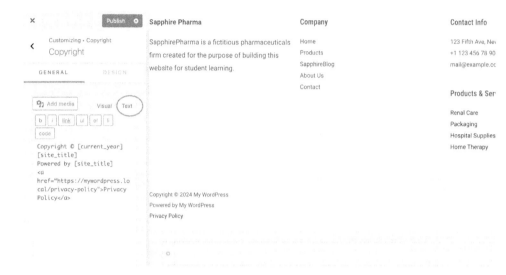

Click on 'Footer Builder' link and then on the 'Copyright' box in the last row of the main part of the page. In the text box of the Astra column on the left, click on the tab that reads 'Text.' See screenshot below.

Copy the following HTML code and paste it after the copyright message in the text box.

<a href="https://mywordpress.local/privacy-policy">Privacy Policy</a>

These strange characters will end up displaying the words Privacy Policy after the copyright message. Not just that, but the words will also serve as a link to the Privacy Policy page you just created.

Click on the 'Publish' button on top of the Astra panel and you're done.

Chapter Summary

- You learned the need and how to optimize images
- You added a favicon to the site

- You added a video to your blog post
- You visited an online resource and published your Privacy Policy page
- You watched the SilentMoves **Videos #24, #25 and #26**

◆ ◆ ◆

11. Making revisions

Once your website's main pages are complete, you will inevitably feel the need to make it better. Changes can be initiated by the client or on our own because we feel something can be improved. These changes may be in the form of text, both headlines and body copy, as well as images.

Perhaps the image size can be made smaller or bigger or changed entirely to something else.

A button is another element where a client may want changes: the text color, the background color, the hover colour, the border curvature, etc.

Let's begin by taking a critical re-look at the site we built.

Editing the mastheads for clarity

We'll start with the home page and look at the masthead.

There is this subheading above the main headline that is sort of blending with the background. Surely, we can improve its legibility. You can sort of read it but the contrast is not very high. The headline has good contrast with the background, so that's alright.

To improve the overall contrast of text against the background image, let's get into our 'Edit with Elementor' mode. Click on the section link on top of the masthead section so that the Elementor panel shows 'Edit Container' or 'Edit Section' depending on your version. It makes no difference to what we are about to do. Click on the Style tab on top.

The best way to handle contrast issues is to add an additional layer called a background overlay to the background. That means in addition to the background image that's there, we give the background a color wash as well. You'll find the Background Overlay section just below the Background section in the Elementor panel. See screenshot below.

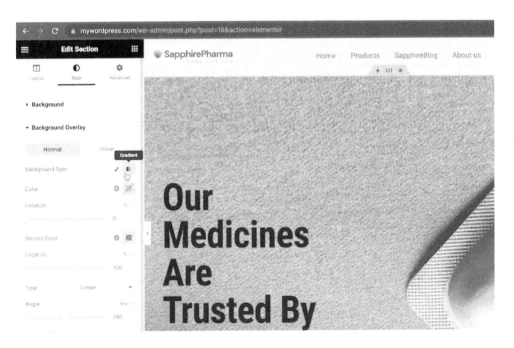

Against the setting Background Type, you'll find two icons, one for 'classic' and another for 'gradient.' (Hover over the icons and you'll see the descriptive text appear.) See screenshot above.

The classic option gives you a choice of colors. If you choose the second option, which is a gradient, you get to choose two colours which fade into each other. Depending on the context, the classic option or the gradient option can be the right one.

The gradient will suit us fine. Click the gradient icon. The Color setting (below the Background Type) gives us the first color setting and the Second Color setting gives us the, duh, second color setting. Choose the first color as black or something close to it from the dropdown list.

The Second Color for some reason has been chosen as red by Elementor itself. Let's keep it that way for the moment. We can change the Angle setting to see what direction the gradient flows. Drag to slider to 110. The gradient now flows from left to right. Which is good for us, as will be evident shortly.

Also drag the Location slider under the first Color (**not** the one under the Second Color) of black to a value of 45. It extends the black to the right so that the transition to red happens a little later on. Now let's change the red by clicking on the red square. A color picker graphic pops up. Drag the second slider at the bottom of the graphic all the way to the left. This controls opacity and our leftward move makes the colour transparent. Which is another way of saying the red has vanished and there is no color overlay here. Which, again, is another way of saying the original colour of the photograph underneath will now show through.

So the first colour is a black which is on the left hand side of the masthead and it transitions into the second colour on the right that is transparent. You can fine-tune the settings by dragging the Location slider under the Second Color to 78 and the overall Opacity slider at the very bottom to 0.45.

The green of the subheading is standing out better now. But, alas, our main headline is now getting merged with the dark background.

Click on the headline. In the Elementor panel, click the Style tab on top. Choose the text colour as white from the dropdown list. That makes our headline's contrast with the background pretty strong.

Remember, as always, to UPDATE your work. Get out of Elementor to view the Home page. Our masthead on the front page looks very good and powerful. See screenshot below.

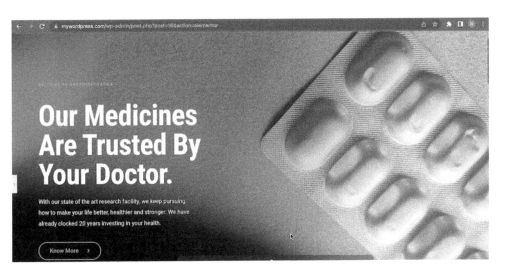

That was a revision worth making, right? Now visit the Products page. You'll see a similar issue of legibility with the masthead there. Follow the exact procedure outlined above and fix the issue with a similar Background Overlay using a gradient. The green button, now illegible, becomes clear and readable once the gradient is in place. You will have to change the text color of both the headline and the text underneath to white.

That should give you great practice in the use of background overlays with gradients. Now to really master this skill, you also have the masthead on the About Us page to practise on—using pretty much the same moves.

I strongly urge you not to breakdown, complain or cry. Website building is a repetitive, lonesome and tedious job. Which is why you can charge a client with vengeance when you get good at this. And repetition builds forbearance besides doing other good things to your soul probably. So cheer up and get the job done! The finished Products masthead should look like something below. You should be able to right away spot the gradient effect like a pro now.

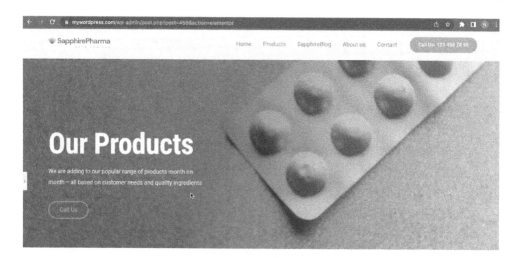

Note: For click-by-click video guidance, watch the **SilentMoves #27 Revise mastheads on site** at new.designWPsite.com/videos. It shows you how to create a gradient effect on background images.

And, while at it, you may want to do pretty much the same thing to the masthead on the About Us page as well.

More revisions to the Home page

Once the mastheads are done, let's head back to the Home page. There are a couple of more revisions to carry out there. Get into the 'Edit with Elementor' mode and scroll down a little. In the legacy section following the masthead, we have the company's founder's image in the left column. Let's say the client wants us to include the founder's name underneath the image, like a photo caption. It is a reasonable request.

Since we have to introduce a new text element below the photograph, we have to be in the Elements mode. Click on the 9-dot cluster at the top right of the Elementor column. Drag the Heading element over to the content pane and drop it under the image. In the title box, replace the words with 'Sam Seth, Founder.'

Go to the Style tab and change the Typography > Size setting to 12 px and in the Style setting below we can choose Italic. These numbers make the name more of a photo caption than a heading. Watch the **SilentMoves Video #28 Add a photo caption** to learn the moves.

Remember to click the UPDATE button below to save the changes. Go down the page to check for any other changes needed. The doctors' testimonials section can do with a minor improvement. Since we are using green here and there as a nice accent color, the three quote marks can be made green to fit our overall theme. See screenshot below.

Open out the Elementor panel (if you've closed it, that is.) Click on the first quote. The Elementor panel reads 'Edit Icon' on top. Click on the

What doctors are saying...

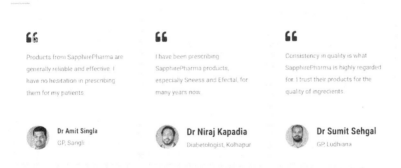

Products from SapphirePharma are generally reliable and effective. I have no hesitation in prescribing them for my patients.

I have been prescribing SapphirePharma products, especially Sneess and Efectal, for many years now.

Consistency in quality is what SapphirePharma is highly regarded for. I trust their products for the quality of ingredients.

Dr Amit Singla
GP, Sangli

Dr Niraj Kapadia
Diabetologist, Kolhapur

Dr Sumit Sehgal
GP, Ludhiana

Style tab and in the Primary Color setting, click on the tiny globe icon to the right to change the color. Choose the green accent color. UPDATE. Do the same thing two more times with the other two quotes in the section.

UPDATE once again. Watch the **SilentMoves Video #28** to understand the moves, click by click. Scroll down the page to continue our scrutiny.

The Famous Brands section feels too scrunched up toward the left with so much empty space on the right. See screenshot below.

Spacing elements horizontally (or even vertically) takes an advanced technique or two, but nothing difficult for a WordPress ninja like you. It's easier to show this technique in action in a video than belabor it in print. Watch the **SilentMoves Video #29 Adjust horizontal spacing** at new.designWPsite.com/videos.

Remember the pink UPDATE button at the bottom. Click. And you're done with the revisions on the page.

Showing the Bottom section only on some pages

If you took a glance at all the pages of the site so far, you will notice that the four-part footer is present on every page of the site. Let's say the client, on review, thinks this is overkill. Let's further say the client is fine

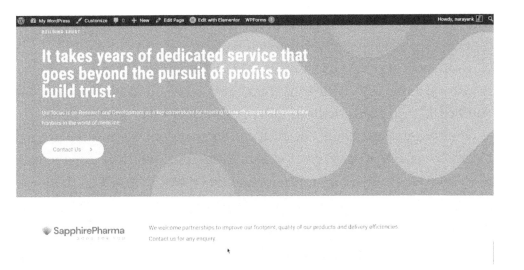

with the two bottom-most footer blocks being there on all pages of the site. These are the copyright block at the very bottom and the company details block just above it.

But they are saying the other two blocks—the green block with a service message and the one below it with a logo and some text asking for partnerships—need not be displayed on all the pages. See the screenshot above. These two blocks do not make sense, they say, on the Blog page (including individual blog posts) as well as the Contact page. Can we remove these two top blocks from these pages please?

If you remember, we got the bottom two footer blocks done in the Astra back end. Since these blocks are not the issue and will remain unchanged on all pages, we don't have to go back there. But the top two footer blocks were done in the Elementor back end. To edit these two blocks, we have to head now to Elementor. And figure out how to remove them from two pages—Blog and Contact—and display them on the other three pages—Home, Products and About.

Unfortunately, **Elementor does not allow us to display these blocks selectively** on some pages and not on others. The workaround is that we first delete these blocks from Elementor so that they show nowhere at all! Clear as mud? Read on, it will all fall into place.

From whichever page you're on at the front end of the site, hover your mouse over the 'Edit with Elementor' link in the admin bar on top, but don't click. Instead, from the dropdown menu, click on **Footer**.

We've done this before. You click on Footer and you see just the two top blocks because they were created with Elementor. Which is exactly what we want. Our aim here is to display the green block as well as the logo-plus-text block below it on three pages of our site but not on the two other pages.

To do that, hover your mouse over the green block section, **right click on the middle icon** of 9-dot cluster on top. From the dropdown menu, click on 'Save as template.' See screenshot below.

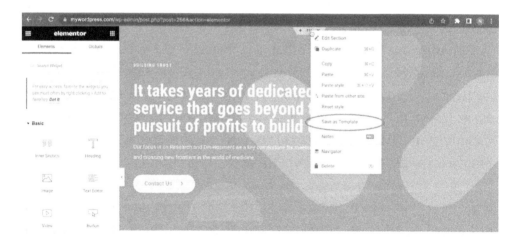

It asks you to give a name for your template. Fill in 'Green block template' and click Save. Why we are creating a template out of a section will become clear in a minute. Similarly, hover your mouse over the logo block section below the green block and right click on its 9-dot cluster and choose 'Save as template.' Name it 'Logo block template' and Save.

Now that the two footer blocks are saved safely somewhere as templates, we can delete them. Hover over the green section and click the 'x' on top to get rid of it. Similarly, delete the logo section as well. The Footer section content panel contains nothing now. Go ahead and click on the pink UPDATE button below to save this nothingness.

When you get out of Elementor by clicking on 'View the page' link, there is nothing to see. Go to the front end. Scroll down the Home page (or any other page of the website for that matter.) The top two blocks are gone forever! Only the bottom two blocks—the company details one and the copyright one—remain.

Have you done something irretrievably dangerous? Not really. It's your job now to visit the 3 pages—Home, About and Products—and add the two template blocks in each of them, one page at a time. And all should be fine. Let's start with the Home page.

Click on 'Edit with Elementor' and scroll down to the bottom of the Home page. Click the **folder icon** in the row of icons. This one links to the Elementor Templates page. See screenshot below.

Click on the My Templates tab on top of the page. Here you will find the templates you saved a few minutes earlier—the Green block template and Logo block template. Let's do the green block first. Click the Insert link at the extreme right. And then click Apply.

Now when you go down the Home page you have the green footer block in place. We need one more footer block. We click on the middle Elementor Templates folder icon again. Go to My Templates tab on top. Insert the Logo block template. Click Apply.

The two blocks are now in place on the Home page. Click on UPDATE button. Get out of Elementor. Check the home page on the front end. All the four footer blocks should now be in place. Hurrah.

In a similar way, proceed to the Products page and do exactly the same thing as above to get the two template blocks in place on that page. And march on to the About Us page and repeat the process for the same results. Feel the tedium creeping into your soul. Enjoy the process of turning from a regular person into a robotic pro.

Note: For click-by-click video guidance, watch the **SilentMoves Video #30 Make section templates for re-use** at <u>new.designWPsite.com/videos.</u> It shows you how to create the 2 Bottom blocks on the Home page.

Click on the pink UPDATE button as always to save your work. Check your work on the front end and ensure the new 4-block footer shows up on the pages it should and doesn't on the pages it shouldn't.

Making this site your own website

With all the pages done and the knowledge of how to do revisions, we've finished our fictitious website on our computer. It's time to turn this website into your own site meant for your business or special interest. You have all the tools and examples and templates waiting to serve you.

Let's briefly recall all you've done so far.

You know by now how to design a page and any section within it. You know how to design any element within any section.

You know how to edit existing template pages, sections, and elements. You also know, that if anything specific you need is not there, how to create it by importing a template block.

You have built the common pages that most websites have: Home, Products, About, Contact, and a Blog. If you need an extra page or two (like a Services page or a Case Studies page) you know Starter Templates can get you started with a page template.

You have two ways of proceeding to create your own site now.

Option 1: Use the pages you've already created as scaffolding. Use them to build your site by replacing the text and content within the sections of each page. Delete or add sections as you please. Build one page at a time. Within that page, build one section at a time. You'd choose this option if the current site we built together is sort of in the broad range of what you want for yourself as a website—in terms of layout, colors, typography and rough pages and sections.

Option 2: Build a new site, your website, from scratch. Keep the Sapphire Pharma site as a reference in the Local by Flywheel app because Local allows you to build multiple sites. You just have to click the '+' button at the bottom left of the Local app to start a new site. As simple as that. Build each page to suit your situation as you keep checking the mywordpress.local site frequently as a guide. The build process will be faster this time round. You've done the stuff before.

Depending on the amount of content you have and the number of pages, you could complete your website in a couple of days. Or a week. Or a month. Or more. It's all perfectly fine.

Take your time to experiment with elements and sections. Between Elementor and Starter Templates, there is a stunning variety of choices. Taking time to discover what fits your purpose isn't a waste. It is an exciting investment of time toward creating something unique for your business.

Once you've got the sections ready and all the pages ready, your site is done!

Chapter Summary

- You edited the masthead sections for legibility through overlays
- You added a caption to a photograph
- You spaced out the Brands section for a balanced layout
- You restricted the display of the 4-block footer section to three pages
- **You took your time and created your own website** using the templates and techniques you've been exposed to
- You watched 4 SilentMoves videos: **Videos #27, 28, 29 and 30**

◆◆◆

12. Migrating to the web

Once you finish your own website on Local by Flywheel, the final step is to transfer it from your private computer to its real home on the worldwide web. Where other people get to visit it, interact with it and get in touch with you. That's the whole point of having a website, right?

You are planting your very own flag in the internet landscape - in the form of your domain name and your domain hosting. Without these, you can't have your WordPress site show its face to the world. What is domain name and domain hosting then?

You're going to come up with a name for your business website. That is your domain name. You're going to make your website live in a folder on the internet that is rented out by someone. That is domain hosting.

Exciting! Even if you're a hobbyist learning about WordPress, you still need a name and hosting for your website. You can't have a website without them.

So decide on a name. It could be as simple as taking your business name and making it into your domain name. Provided no one else in the world has already taken it, of course. There are no duplicate domain names on the internet.

How to choose your site name

Important Note: For this step, choose a real name for your real business, not the pharma firm we're pretending to be. Because your real website is ready on your own computer by now and we need a good domain name for it.

For example, if you have a plumbing service called Joe Blackburn Plumbing it can easily become your domain name by 'crushing' it all together: joeblackburnplumbing.com. (You can't have spaces in a domain name, unfortunately.)

Be easy to remember and relevant. Don't use hyphens in your domain name. Hyphens make it difficult for people to type in. For visual clarity you can use a mix of capital and lower case letters to separate the words: JoeBlackburnPlumbing.com

That makes for easier reading by humans. The internet doesn't care one way or the other.

The point is even if your visitor forgets to type the capitalization in the exact places you intended or forgets to use capital letters totally, people will still reach your site. Provided the overall spelling is correct, of course.

On the other hand, you may not want a domain name that mimics your business name. That's fine too. You may have options on the table such as:

plumbingforless.com

plumbexpress.com

yourlocalplumber.com

topplumbinginmiami.com

And so on. You get the picture. It's totally up to you to decide the kind of name you want for your website. Brainstorm with your spouse, colleague, or friend.

Once you have a domain name, you have to purchase it from a **domain name registrar** so that the internet will then recognize it and treat it as a valid address. It is a one-step process, really. You purchase it, it gets registered automatically.

We will be checking shortly if a website with your desired name already exists. It happens fairly often, by the way. It's prudent to keep a few variations or options ready as your possible domain name.

From where do you purchase a domain name? From the same place you will purchase your domain hosting. Let's head there.

There are many reputed hosting companies out there: GoDaddy, Hostinger, Dreamhost, Bluehost, Siteground and so many more. I'm recommending Hostinger to you because I personally use it a lot. I recently moved 50 of my client sites to Hostinger because I found the price-performance value excellent.

If you prefer to go with Godaddy or Bluehost or anyone else, that's fine too. But the display screens you will see in this book will be different from vendor to vendor. Obviously, I can't show you every possible screenshot from every possible vendor. I'll stick to showing you how to get it done on Hostinger.

The good news is most hosting companies have a similar enough registration process that you won't find it difficult. Once you get the hang of what to do on the Hostinger site, it's more or less the same with any other vendor.

Go to Hostinger.com. If you're in a country that is not the US, click on 'English' in the top left corner. A whole list of countries appears for you to choose from. I suggest you choose your country from the list because Hostinger has local deals going on all the time.

For the purpose of this book, I will use India as an example. You can choose the country of your choice.

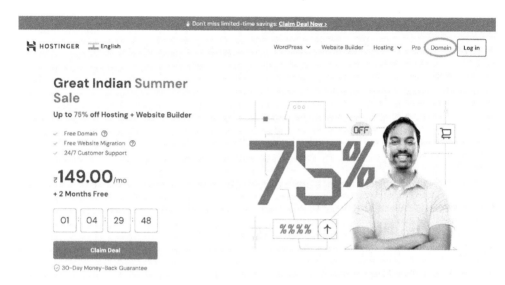

From the main menu on top, click on 'Domain' (or 'Domains' as it reads in some countries). See screenshot above. It takes you to the Domain Name Search screen. Let's check if the domain name we want is available. When I type in 'sapphirepharma.com' in the search box and click on the Search button, it tells me the domain name is taken.

So I put in my next option 'pharmasapphire.com.' Success! The domain name is available. Try out your domain name(s) here and see what wins for you. Once you have it in the bag, we move on to domain hosting.

Get yourself some domain hosting

In the main menu, click on Hosting and in the dropdown menu, click 'Web Hosting.' Scroll down a bit and you'll see the many hosting plans on offer. The names of the hosting plans keep changing all the time and depending on when you visit the site, the names you see could be different.

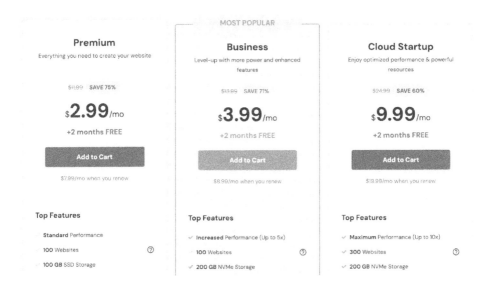

Premium

Everything you need to create your website

$11.99 SAVE 75%

$**2.99**/mo

+2 months FREE

Add to Cart

$7.99/mo when you renew

Top Features

Standard Performance

100 Websites ⑦

100 GB SSD Storage

Business

Level-up with more power and enhanced features

$13.99 SAVE 71%

$**3.99**/mo

+2 months FREE

Add to Cart

$8.99/mo when you renew

Top Features

✓ Increased Performance (Up to 5x)

✓ 100 Websites ⑦

✓ 200 GB NVMe Storage

Cloud Startup

Enjoy optimized performance & powerful resources

$24.99 SAVE 60%

$**9.99**/mo

+2 months FREE

Add to Cart

$19.99/mo when you renew

Top Features

✓ Maximum Performance (Up to 10x)

✓ 300 Websites ⑦

✓ 200 GB NVMe Storage

Right now, I'm seeing the options Premium, Business and Cloud Start-up. See screenshot above.

The Premium plan (the cheapest one by whatever name it may be called) is good enough for us. Note that by default you can build up to 100 websites with this plan.

If you're going to be a future freelancer or you want to start building sites for your friends and relatives for fun or practise, this option is great.

Click on the Add to Cart button. Pay up as you would on any online shopping site. And you are now the proud owner of your products: a domain name and domain hosting.

Once you purchase your name and hosting, log in using your username and password for the site. Click on 'Websites' in the main menu on top. You will see your site listed here. See screenshot below. I have a handful of my client sites listed here, but you'll see just the one you purchased. Click on the Manage button to get to the Hostinger dashboard for your site. You can manage all the settings related to your site from here.

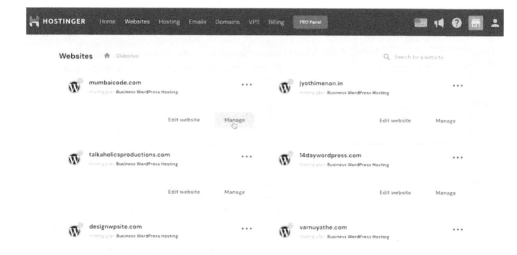

Installing WordPress

On the Hostinger dashboard page, click on WordPress in the left column. In the submenu that appears, click on Overview. In the main content panel on the right, scroll down till you see 'Install WordPress.' Click on the Install button.

As you may remember (or may not remember, that's fine too), when we used Local by Flywheel to install WordPress on your computer, it went behind the scenes to wordpress.org and downloaded the software and installed it. We didn't need to go to WordPress.org ourselves to procure the software.

Similarly, Hostinger now does the running around for us to get the latest version of WordPress software and install it on our site. Once this is done, on the Hostinger dashboard page (reachable from the Websites menu item on top of the page), notice the purple button that reads 'Admin panel.' See screenshot below. Clicking it takes you to the **WordPress back end** of your brand new site on the web bearing the domain name you gave.

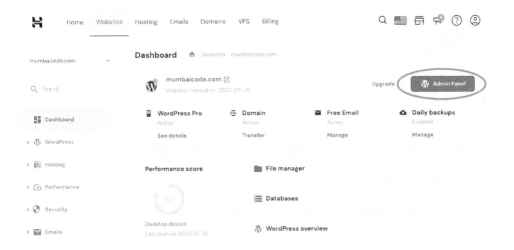

The back end view of a WordPress site should be so familiar to you by now. It's good to remember that this one, bearing your very own domain name, represents a totally empty site. If you see any red badges in the black, left column informing you of updates needed for the site, ignore them. We are going to be filling out the empty site with the contents of the completed site on our computer. Once that is done, we'll check if any updates are still needed and get them done then.

Click on Plugins in the left column. You'll find that Hostinger has populated the plugins page with a set of 'helpful' plugins. We don't need all of them. Delete Akismet, Hello Dolly and WP-Forms Lite plugins (and anything else) the usual way: click on the Delete button below the plugin name.

Watch the SilentMoves **Video #31 Prepare online site for migration** to set up your WordPress site and make it ready to 'receive' your Local site.

Migrating the Local site to the web

Let's get back to our original site, **mywordpress.local on your computer.** Start up Local by Flywheel app, choose our site name in the left column, and click on WP Admin button to the top right.

Remember, just to be clear, we are dealing with two distinct websites now. Don't get confused. Keep your wits about. One is mywordpress.local which lives in your computer and full of content that is your website. And the other is the totally empty yourwebsitename.com site sitting pretty and vacant on the worldwide web inside of a hosting company called Hostinger.

Right now, we are at the backend of the totally full and finished Local by Flywheel site in the browser. Got your bearings, right? Click on Plugins in the left column. You'll see all our plugins including Starter Templates, Elementor, etc. Let's add one more new plugin here.

Click the Add New button right on top of the page next to the page title of Plugins. You are now in the vast WordPress repository of plugins. Type in 'all in one wp migration' in the search box. The plugin will appear along with many others.

Check the plugin information in the plugin box. 5 million plus active installations, over 7000 recommendations, ratings, last updated recently, and it is compatible with our version of WordPress. All good. Install this by clicking the Install button. Activate it by clicking the Activate button. Routine stuff. You are now back on the Plugins page. (Or else, if you see a greyed out Active button, click on Plugins > Installed plugins in the black column on the left.)

Look now for a new item in the menu listing in the left column: All-in-One WP Migration. Hover the mouse over it and from the submenu, click on Export.

Click on the green 'Export To' box. The dropdown menu offers many options but we are going to choose the first one: File. It begins its job straightaway with an info box 'Preparing to export.' Once a blinking box that says 'Download mywordpress.local' appears, click on it. This saves the exported file (containing everything in your site) in your computer's Downloads folder. Close the box now. We have our whole local website inside of a single file now.

Go over to the **back end of your empty online site**. Install the All-in-One WP Migration plugin here too. Once installed and activated, look for the All-in-One WP Migration item in the listing in the left column. Hover your mouse over it. In the submenu that appears, click on **Import**. Click on the 'Import From' box. Choose the first option of File. Locate the file you imported from the local site earlier. The import process will start now. Click on the Proceed button when the import is over. Click on the Finish button when it appears.

Go to Settings in the left column and click on Permalinks from the submenu. To our surprise, instead of taking us to the Permalinks page, it logs us out of our website! This is fine. Login again with the **username and password of our original site** that we created with Local by Flywheel.

So now we are back at the back end of our online site. Click on Settings > Permalinks. Check that 'Post name' is the chosen option and click the Save button at the bottom of the page. If it isn't, select 'Post name' and click the Save button.

Go to the front end now for another surprise—this time, a pleasant one. Our original site's Home page is what we see now with everything in place. As you check page after page, you realize this online site is an exact replica of the one you have in your computer. You are online! Hello, world.

To watch a step-by-step video, watch the **SilentMoves Video #32 Migrate from Local to online** at new.designWPsite.com/videos.

Basically, you've moved over the local site onto the web successfully. Migration complete. You must be a champ. This is the perfect time to let Google know you have finished. Yours is no longer a secret website eking its lonely life inside your computer. It's a proud, legit citizen of the world wide web, no less. To proclaim this in emphatic terms, do the following.

Go to the Settings link in the back end and go through each of General, Writing, Reading, etc. sub-items. Change all details to suit your real site now, as necessary.

Especially, click on **Settings > Reading**. Click the checkbox at the bottom of the page against 'Search engine visibility' to untick it. You are now ready to let the Google into your site and index it in its records.

Chapter Summary

- You learned how to choose a domain name for your business
- You purchased a domain name and domain hosting
- You installed WordPress on your domain host
- You exported your local site to a file
- You imported the file to your online site
- You watched **SilentMoves Videos #31 and 32**

NOTE: From here on, you'll make any further changes on the online site. Including text and images, plugin and theme updates, new blog posts, etc. So what happens to the original site in your computer? You can delete it or keep it as a fond memory of the first site you ever built. Your call.

◆◆◆

13. Finishing touches

In this final chapter of learning WordPress with Elementor/Astra, we will talk about important finishing touches and techniques to your online site. These are essential to most websites and you should include them in your own website once you learn how.

• Integrating a popular app like Calendly on your site
• Installing 3 important plugins for your site's safety, speed, and backup (important!)
• Testing your site's speed (why and how)

Let's start with the Calendly app for appointments.

Taking appointments on the website

Generally speaking, most sites have a contact form on their Contact page. A visitor gets there either from the main menu and/or gets directed from other pages through a call-to-action button.

Typically these buttons read 'Contact Us' or 'Get in touch' or something similar. Clicking on them gets you to the Contact page.

These days, an option that is becoming popular is to have the button read 'Make an appointment' or 'Let's talk' or something similar.

This button link does not go to the Contact page on our site. **It goes to a third-party appointment site like calendly.com.** Once there, on your Calendly page, your visitor can choose from an online calendar and fix their appointments with you for a certain day and time.

Calendly allows you as the site owner to set up date and time slots that are convenient to you. The visitor has to merely choose one of those defined slots. Appointment fixed! Just to be clear, Calendly has nothing to do with WordPress; it is an independent app on its own. You can use it without even having a website to fix your appointments.

But it's nice to integrate the app with your website. Your visitor, already on your site, gets the opportunity to click a button and seamlessly fix an appointment with you at a convenient day and time.

To make the integration possible, you have to have a free account with calendly.com. You may already have a Calendly account. If not, it's a fairly

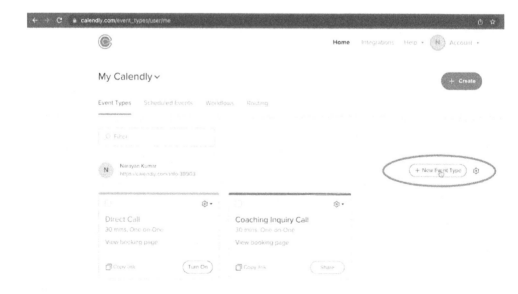

simple process to register. Once registered, you create a New Event Type in calendly.com (see screenshot above) to set up your time slots when you're free to take calls from potential customers. You can name the Event ('Web Enquiry'), set up custom dates and times, duration of the call, ask for the visitor's phone number and email beforehand, decide if they should call you or you'd call them and other details.

Once set up, the Event box will show up on your front page on the Calendly site (along with other Event boxes you may have set up.) Inside the Event box click on the 'Copy link' link at the bottom left. See screenshot below. This is the link to your appointments page you need to carry over to your website.

On the website, the header on top has a green button to the extreme right that reads 'Fix Appointment.' Since the header is there on every page of the website, this button is a good place for an always-visible call to action button. We make the button hold the link to our appointments page on Calendly. Let's do it.

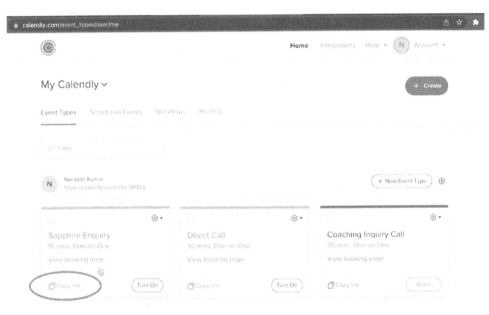

As noted earlier, editing the header is done within Astra, not Elementor. See the Global Settings chapter if you want a refresher.

Click the 'Customize' link in the black admin bar from any page on the front end. Click on Header Builder and then on Button. In the Link box, delete the '#' that's there and paste in the Calendly link you saved earlier. A simple Ctrl-V or Cmd-V should do the job.

To test if this button works the way we expect it to, either log out or open a new incognito window (from the File menu) if you're on Chrome. This is so that you're no longer the admin looking at the site, but a regular, random visitor. Type in [yourwebsitename.com] in the address bar. You'll see the Home page as your visitor would. Click the green button on the header that reads 'Fix Appointment.' You'll be taken to your Calendly appointments page to fix your appointment with the company.

The integration is done.

3 basic hygiene plugins for your site

One of the last things you should do on your website after everything is done is to safeguard it. You want **to provide a firewall** around it making it tough for evil bots to break in. You want to ensure your **site loads fast** and doesn't dawdle for long with clicks.

And you want to **take periodic backups** of your site and store them somewhere handy. In the event of—God forbid!—a site crash, you can always restore the original site from the latest backup.

For reasons of safety, speed and backing up, I consider the 3 plugins below as basic hygiene. Your site shouldn't go out and present itself to the world without these in place.

There are other options to these plugins—and good ones at that—but I think these 3 are truly top of the class. Free versions of these plugins are sufficient for our use.

Wordfence for security

The installation of this plugin is like any other. In the WordPress backend, click on **Plugins > Add New** and when taken to the WordPress plugin library, type in 'wordfence' in the search box.

When it appears, click on 'Install' and then 'Activate.' Usual stuff, right? You're taken to the back end. Wordfence is now listed in the black left column. Hover your mouse on it and click Dashboard in the submenu that appears. You'll get an info box telling you to get your license. Click on

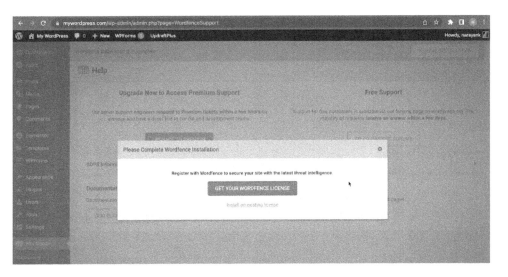

the button. See screenshot above.

It takes you to the Wordfence website, where you are required to register. Choose the Free Option. In the next info box click on the 'I'm OK waiting for 30 days...' link unless you want the premium (paid) version. The free version is good for our work. Fill in your email and tick the checkbox so that you can click on the Register button.

You'll receive an email with the license key. Click on the link in the mail to take you to your site's back end with an info box asking you to complete the installation. Fill in your email and the license key. Click on the Install License button.

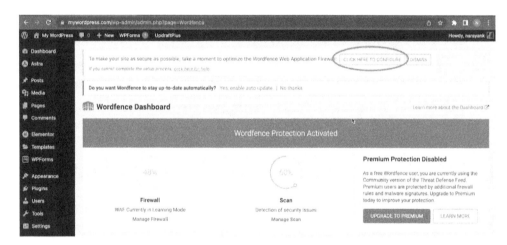

In the Firewall message at the top of the page, click on the button that reads 'Click Here To Configure.' See screenshot above. Click on 'Continue' button in the popup box and you're done setting up the firewall.

Wordfence is a pretty deep and complex plugin. But we all have to start somewhere. Now that the firewall is in place, there's one more thing you can do. Under the Wordfence item in the left column, click on Scan in the submenu. Click on the 'Start New Scan' button. See screenshot below.

The scan takes a few minutes to complete as it scans your WordPress installation for malware and other bad things. You'll get a series of tick

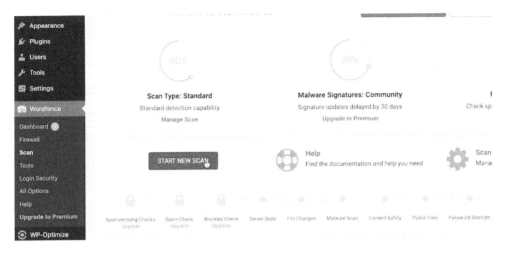

marks to tell you your site is clean. (You should run this scan periodically to keep your site clean.)

Note: For click-by-click video guidance, watch the **SilentMoves Video #33: Wordfence for security** at new.designWPsite.com/videos. It shows you how to install and use the Wordfence plugin on your website.

WP-Optimize for caching (speed)

Similarly, install and activate the free plugin WP-Optimize from the plugin library. Once you're back in the WordPress plugins page, you will see the new plugin listed among all the others you have. Click on 'Settings' under the plugin name.

From the menu on the top right, click on 'Database' to optimize the database for your site. Click on the blue button that reads 'Run all selected optimizations.' Wait for a few moments till it's done.

Click on 'Cache' from the top menu. Switch on 'Enable page caching'. Click on 'Save changes' button at the bottom. You're all set with this plugin.

Note: For click-by-click video guidance, watch the **SilentMoves Video #34 WP-Optimize for speed** at <u>new.designWPsite.com/videos</u>. It shows you how to install the WP-Optimize plugin for use on your website.

Updraft Plus for backing up your site

Install and activate Updraft Plus from the plugins library as usual.

Once you see the plugin in your plugins list, click on 'Settings' under the plugin name. You will land in the Backup/Restore tab of the plugin's dashboard. Click on the 'Settings' tab. From the first drop-down menu for files backup, choose 'Weekly' and retain 3 backups. Use a similar setting for the second dropdown menu for database backup.

Below, you will see a list of **possible storage options** you can use for backing up your website. The free version of Updraft Plus, the one we're using, allows only one of these storage options to be chosen.

Google Drive is the popular one and almost everyone has their own drive with their stuff on it. Click on 'Google Drive' and then go all the way down to click on the 'Save Changes' button. You will be asked to sign in to your Google account if you aren't signed in already.

Follow the instructions and your Google drive will be 'connected' with your Updraft Plus plugin. Click on the blue Backup Now button to save a backup of your site to your Google drive. Once done, every week, your site will be backed up automatically from now on. That should be reassuring.

The last 3 saved backups will be preserved, so you don't take up inordinate space on your drive. You can breathe easy now. Your site is safely stored.

Watch the **SilentMoves Video #35 Updraft Plus for backups** for help if you need it.

Testing your site speed

Once you are happy with your site build, you should test its speed. A popular and reliable measure of site speed is **GTMetrix**. Go to gtmetrix.com and put your site URL in the box and hit 'Test your site' button.

You will get to see the key metrics. If everything is green, you are in a good place. You are well and truly done. Watch the **SilentMoves Video #36 GTMetrix to test site speed** to get the moves.

Chapter Summary

- You integrated your website with a third-party app Calendly
- You installed plugins for security, speed, and backups
- You tested your site for speed
- You watched **SilentMoves Videos #33 to #36**

◆◆◆

14. Where to next?

W here to now?
You have solid, practical knowledge now to build your own website with WordPress and Elementor. There is always more stuff to learn, of course, but you have an adequate head start.

You have learned the skills to put together **pages** of a WordPress website. In turn, every page taught you how to handle the Elementor **sections** within them. And the sections taught you how to create and edit the Elementor **elements** (blocks or widgets) within.

You did all this with the help of the Elementor plug-in along with the Astra theme and another plugin called Starter Templates.

For some of you running active businesses, this amount of learning to get you a professional, full-featured website will feel sufficient. For others, this may only be whetting your appetite to learn more.

If you are the latter kind, here is a series of exploratory steps you may wish to take.

One, **learn more about Elementor** (free version.) Even without Starter Templates, Elementor can be your powerful ally if you use it well. I particularly recommend Elementor's own set of videos on YouTube. It is a short course of 8 videos that introduces you to the free version of

Elementor used in conjunction with their own, light-weight Hello theme (instead of Astra.)

The Hello theme performs pretty much the same function that we saw Astra do. Mainly, it helped us access and edit the header and footer regions to our satisfaction. Something that the free version of Elementor does not allow us to.

This course is accessible here: https://www.youtube.com/watch?v=icTcREd1tAg

You will receive good design suggestions as well as understand more about Elementor's start-from-scratch page design without using Starter Templates. That will help you understand the features of Elementor in depth. You will also learn about responsive websites, the ability to make your site respond and adapt itself to the device it is viewed on.

Two, you may consider **buying Elementor Pro** for its additional features. The price is $59 (annual subscription for a single website, at the time of writing) which is frankly nothing much considering the value you get.

Elementor Pro comes with the Theme Builder feature which lets you design everything on the site - including headers and footers, blog posts, etc. You get more freedom in designing your form or forms on the site. You receive, as you expect to, more templates and blocks you can make use of. Plus, if you're getting into building an e-commerce website, the Pro version gives you lots of integration features with WooCommerce.

Three, as the months go by, the traffic to your site will increase. You may wish to know who these visitors are, what exactly they are looking for on your website, how long they are spending on which pages and so on. You have to get **Google Analytics on your side (or equivalent)** to help you with visitor information.

It's a free service and is integrated through one of many plugins available. It's easy to set up. At some point in the future, it is inevitable that you will need to get and understand these numbers. As usual, YouTube is your friend and you can search it for how to install Google Analytics on your WordPress site.

A good alternative, and simpler to use, is a plugin called Clicky. Just install it and follow the instructions. Most people, including me, find it a lot less geeky and a breeze to use.

Four, get interested in **Search Engine Optimization**. Any business needs traffic. Understanding how to get more traffic for your website involves a good understanding of SEO. The basics are fairly simple. Learn how to get a firm grasp of the keywords at the heart of your business and how to put them to good use.

Five, the simplest to do, learn **how to update themes and plugins**. As you visit the backend of your website over time, keep an eye for those themes and plugins that require updating. WordPress will put out messages in the back end telling you what needs updating including updates to itself. Your job is to pay heed, head over to the concerned theme or plugin and click on the link that says 'update.'

This task is something you must perform diligently by checking the back end of your site at least once a week, even if you have nothing else to do there. Good maintenance can save you big trouble. Also, know that WordPress itself undergoes changes a few times in a year and will require periodic updating (very important!).

Here's wishing you years and years of a great looking website that brings you fruitful results. All the best!

◆ ◆ ◆

May I ask you for a small favor?

At the outset, I want to give you a big thanks for taking out time to read this book. I totally appreciate this.

I hope you got more than a few actionable steps to start you off on building your own website using WordPress and Elementor. You will get better with time, rest assured.

Can I ask for 30 seconds more of your time?

I'd love it if you could leave a positive review about the book. Reviews may not matter to big-name authors; but they're a tremendous help for authors like me, who are relatively new on the block. They encourage other folks to take a chance on my books.

To put it straight– reviews are the life blood for any author.

Please leave your review on my book's Amazon page: "The New Way To Design Your Own Website With WordPress." Or you can search there for the author's name: Narayan Kumar.

It will just take a few minutes of your time, but will tremendously help me to reach out to more people.

Thanks for your support to my work. And I'd love to see your review.

♦ ♦ ♦

Coming soon... Design Your Own Website With WordPress - *Volume Two*

Coming shortly!

Make an investment in building your business. I'm planning a VOLUME TWO to the Design Your Own Website series to teach a professional website build with advanced features. It will go beyond the basics that this book (and the earlier one) covers.

The writing of VOLUME TWO got pushed when I decided to write this current version, **The New Way**, as a follow-up to the earlier Design Your Own Website book. I thought this approach would be more useful—of starting with one's own computer and learning to build a WordPress site immediately rather than starting with and wading through the geekery of getting domain names, hosting spaces and all the rest before getting down to building a website (as in Book I.)

Besides, using this approach to build a different website would be of benefit to users who got something fresh to work on. It justified the publication of a new book.

With **Volume Two**, I plan to leave behind the free world of Elementor, explored in some detail in both my books (Design Your Own Website With WordPress and The New Way to Design Your Own Website With WordPress). Instead, I will teach you how best to use **Elementor Pro** for greater flexibility in designing your site your way, including e-commerce sites.

For a small business, an annual outlay of an Elementor Pro subscription ($69) is nothing but the benefits are huge. The power to fine-tune your content and styling is vast. Volume Two covers key aspects like:

- Setting up Elementor Pro
- Importing Elementor Pro's ready to use **styling kits** for an overall, killer look for your site
- **Better blog design** choices
- Learning advanced features like **animated headlines, sliders,** social buttons, etc.
- Setting up your own, **domain-based email** using Google
- Using **Theme Builder** to create custom headers and footers, single post layouts, archive pages, etc.
- Using **Pop-up Builder** to create custom pop-up windows for lead generation, announcements, promotions, etc.
- Learning **motion effects** and on-screen animation effects
- Introduction to **building an e-commerce website**
- Accessing a **larger library of widgets,** pro templates and blocks for more design freedom
- Using the Form widget instead of a third-party plugin for a site form
- Integrating with marketing tools like MailChimp, ConvertKit, etc. for **email marketing campaigns** to collect emails of site visitors and send them batch mails
- SilentMoves videos to illustrate all key steps
- And much more!

Keep yourself updated on the release date of Volume Two by registering at new.designWPsite.com.

Note: If you need more practice at building a site, you can get my earlier book **Design Your Own Website With WordPress**, available at Amazon. It helps you build, step by step, a consultant-coach's website from scratch with its own requirements and layouts. You have the same help there too with sample content downloads and SilentMoves videos to help you with the clicks. Since you now know how to build using Local by Flywheel, I suggest ignoring the book's earlier chapters on working with an online site and use Local instead. Get good practise in building a site for a service business, like a career coach. That's the bulk of the book in any case. Have a blast!

◆ ◆ ◆

About The Author

Narayan Kumar is a senior communications professional with three decades of advertising experience. He is a copywriter and designer who kept pace with the digital medium. As a director of his agency, he is well versed in web design basics and build technologies including Ruby on Rails. But his favorite weapon of choice is WordPress for all the freedom it gives him in design and flexibility. It also allows his clients and their teams to easily visit the admin section and make editorial changes at will without any coding knowledge.

Narayan currently heads his WordPress consulting venture, Blue Mountain Code. Along with his wife, he consults, builds, writes, and designs anything and everything that has to do with WordPress and brand building for small business.

new.designWPsite.com is this book's website for downloads and updates

www.bluemountaincode.com is the author's business website for consulting and projects

All sample content for use along with this book can be downloaded from the author's website: new.designWPsite.com/downloads

All help videos supplementing the instructions in this book can be viewed on the author's website: new.designWPsite.com/videos

◆◆◆

www.ingramcontent.com/pod-product-compliance
Lightning Source LLC
LaVergne TN
LVHW022124060326
832903LV00063B/3632